Colin Robson

Experiment, Design and Statistics in Psychology

Second Edition

Penguin Books

Penguin Books Ltd, Harmondsworth, Middlesex, England
Viking Penguin Inc., 40 West 23rd Street, New York, New York 10010, U.S.A.
Penguin Books Australia Ltd, Ringwood, Victoria, Australia
Penguin Books Canada Limited, 2801 John Street, Markham, Ontario, Canada L3R 1B4
Penguin Books (N.Z.) Ltd, 182–190 Wairau Road, Auckland 10, New Zealand

First published in Penguin Books 1973
Reprinted 1974, 1975, 1977, 1979, 1981, 1982
Second edition 1983
Reprinted in Pelican Books 1985
Reprinted 1985, 1987

Reproduced, printed and bound in Great Britain by
Hazell Watson & Viney Limited,
Member of the BPCC Group,
Aylesbury, Bucks
Set in Linotron Times by
Rowland Phototypesetting Ltd, Bury St Edmunds, Suffolk

To my wife

Contents

How to select a test

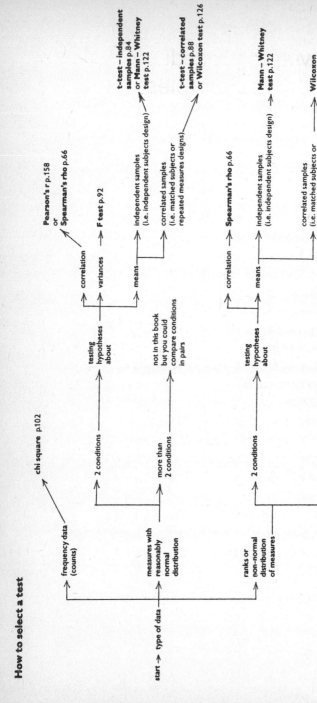

start → type of data

frequency data (counts) → **chi square** p.102

measures with reasonably normal distribution — **testing hypotheses about**:
- correlation → **Pearson's r** p.158 or **Spearman's rho** p.66
- variances → **F test** p.92
- means:
  - independent samples (i.e. independent subjects design) → **t-test – independent samples** p.84 or **Mann – Whitney test** p.122
  - correlated samples (i.e. matched subjects or repeated measures designs) → **t-test – correlated samples** p.88 or **Wilcoxon test** p.126

more than 2 conditions → not in this book but you could compare conditions in pairs

ranks or non-normal distribution of measures — **testing hypotheses about**:
- correlation → **Spearman's rho** p.66
- means:
  - independent samples (i.e. independent subjects design) → **Mann – Whitney test** p.122
  - correlated samples (i.e. matched subjects or repeated measures designs) → **Wilcoxon test** p.126

more than 2 conditions → not in this book but you could compare conditions in pairs

Step-by-step procedures with worked examples

Editorial foreword

There are basic skills which are essential for progress in a variety of subjects, but which often prove to be stumbling blocks for people who otherwise have the necessary ability and motivation. Particularly is this true of various branches of mathematics, especially statistics. Many pure and applied scientists, and non-scientists too, need to have a working knowledge of statistics, and in a large number of cases they develop a block against the subject. A common reaction is to argue that the actual work can be left to the professional statisticians 'as long as I know where to go for help'. This is rather like arguing 'I need not make my car safe because I know where to go for first aid.' The planning of one's own work, and one's appraisal of other people's, is immeasurably improved by *first hand* experience of statistical techniques.

I did not think it was possible to write an introduction to statistics which was positively entertaining, but Colin Robson has succeeded. He is a psychologist, and the book is a result of courses given to psychology students, but the techniques which he teaches are the basic ones used in a variety of disciplines. Especially important is the way the author leads the reader into working out examples, because statistics is one of those subjects in which the learner can develop insight as a result of practice. Familiarity becomes a pretty good substitute for a knowledge of the underlying mathematics.

People who understand the mathematics, but can also teach the techniques in a simple way, are difficult to find. Colin Robson says he is not a Statistician (with a capital S). He is however a very good teacher.

B.M.F.

Preface

For a number of years I have lectured on summer courses in experimental psychology, statistics and experimental design at the University of London for external students registered for degrees in psychology. Students on these courses were of extremely varied mathematical background which meant that, if all were to follow the work in statistics, little beyond elementary algebra could be assumed. The core of this book consists of material from lectures and hand-outs presented for these courses. It has been pretty well pre-tested in that the students on these courses were excellent at giving feedback if a particular approach was unclear. While a lot of ground is covered in a relatively small number of words, many of the basic concepts are introduced and reintroduced at several points in the book. This redundancy, which springs from the fact that the material was originally intended for aural consumption, is, I hope, helpful rather than the converse. Similarly no attempt has been made to alter the informal style in which the material was originally presented.

I am not a statistician, as may perhaps be revealed to any of that breed who read this. However, I have had a good deal of enjoyment in initiating students – particularly those who shy away from anything mathematical and have to be handled with a very loose rein – into the mysteries and delights of designing and analysing experiments.

I am indebted to the literary executor of the late Sir Ronald A. Fisher, F.R.S., to Dr Frank Yates, F.R.S., and to Oliver & Boyd, Edinburgh, for permission to reprint Table 33 from their book *Statistical Tables for Biological, Agricultural and Medical Research*.

Preface

Finally, I would like to thank the students mentioned above, my wife for her attempts to tame my written style, and Pat Needham and Susan Moorhouse for expert and speedy assistance with typing.

Colin Robson
1973

Preface to Second Edition

Since preparing the first edition of this book I have gained further experience in teaching the introductory statistics and experimental design course, mainly with students on the Behavioural Sciences degree at Huddersfield Polytechnic. They have been no less vociferous than the external psychology degree students of London University in indicating any lack of clarity and their resulting confusion. The modifications in this second edition are largely resulting from this interaction.

In particular I am now no longer persuaded by statisticians' arguments as to the superiority of Kendall's tau over Spearman's rho and feel that the computational simplicity of the latter gives it the edge. Pearson's Correlation coefficient is covered in an Appendix as it figures in several introductory syllabuses and is useful in introducing ideas needed in more advanced work.

The example used to introduce basic notions about experiments has been brought up-to-date and there is a somewhat more serious attempt to explain the concept of probability. Otherwise the basic approach in the first edition has been retained. I have been very grateful for the feedback I have received both face to face and in written form. Some modifications arise from such comments although I have resisted advice that the book might concern itself more with issues to do with tests and testing, with reliability, validity etc., primarily to keep it as slim as possible.

Much of the drudgery associated with computing, say, a t-test, is removed by using the calculator and I would urge all those using this book not only to get a calculator but also to acquire some facility in its use. Given the rapid changes in this area it is not very helpful to recommend specific models. A square root and a memory function are useful but I feel that starting out by using the more complex programmable calculators tends to defeat the object of understanding something of the basis of the various tests. Given that understanding there is, of course, a lot to be said for using more powerful machines. Micro-computers have much to offer in this connection and the reader may be interested to know that the statistical tests covered in this book, together with more complex tests, are incorporated in the SUPASTAT programs developed by one of my colleagues[1] for use on the 380 Z and Apple micro-computers.

1. For details contact Roger Eglen, 17 Tanhouse Park, Hipperholme, Halifax, West Yorkshire HX3 8HP

Note to the 1985 reprint: The opportunity has been taken to correct some errors which crept into the second edition and to recast Table C of Appendix 3 in the light of helpful criticism.

1 Introduction

What this book tries to do

My aim is to help you to design, carry out, analyse and interpret experiments. The bias is towards techniques that are commonly used in psychology and education, although there is no real reason why they should be restricted to these particular subject matters. As far as statistical tests are concerned, the book is a 'cook-book'. It has been designed to guide you to the right recipe – the statistical test appropriate to the problem – and then carry you through the steps of the recipe with a maximum of detail. The intention is not to train statisticians, but to give people doing experiments the statistical tools they need. Formulae are not derived, and the only mathematical requirement is some elementary algebra, together with the ability to substitute numbers into formulae. As mentioned in the preface to this edition, an electronic calculator together with some facility in its use will enable you to cut out a lot of the drudgery once thought to be an inescapable part of statistical analysis.

However, the book is not just a 'cook-book'. Apart from the fact that such a compendium of statistical recipes would be deadly boring and hardly likely to kindle any flames of interest or enthusiasm, it would not be able to fulfil the aim of the book. If you are to select a particular statistical test, you need to appreciate what the test is capable of doing, why it is that that particular test is appropriate and others are not. In order to achieve this, some kind of understanding, even if only at an intuitive level, is essential. Hence an attempt is made to talk around and lead up to the tests in such a way that that kind of understanding has a chance to develop.

In addition to this, there is a very close relationship between the design of an experiment and the appropriate statistical analysis.

There are many sad stories of students, burning to carry out an experimental project, who end up with a completely unanalysable mishmash of data. They wanted to get on with it, and thought that they could leave thoughts of analysis until after the experiment. They were wrong. Statistical analysis and experimental design must be considered together and, whilst there are broad principles of experimental design which will be covered, they cannot easily be reduced to recipes guaranteed for every eventuality.

Using statistics is no insurance against producing rubbish. Badly used, misapplied statistics simply allow one to produce quantitative rubbish rather than qualitative rubbish.

Limitations of the book

Do not get the impression that all the techniques on statistical analysis are to be laid at your feet in the next chapters. This is not the case. You will be given a severely limited range of techniques. What I do hope, however, is that you will be able to take the questions that you are interested in and turn them into experiments which can be analysed meaningfully by one or more tests out of this repertoire. This will not always be possible, and you may well find that in trying to fit your experiment into the strait-jacket of one of these techniques, so much violence is done to the original idea that it is not worth doing.

One of my main aims is to enable you to recognize situations like this. The strategy then is either to yell for help or to sit down and try to approach the problem from a different direction – one which will allow the techniques to be used. But do not be discouraged; it is surprising how many interesting questions can be investigated in simply designed experiments for which the straightforward statistical tests described here are adequate and appropriate.

Requirements from the reader

The main requirement, virtually the only requirement, is that *you should want to do experiments*. If you are certain that you do not want to do experiments, then you are wasting your time reading this book and should pack it in. It is true that a knowledge of statistics and experimental design enables one to understand and evaluate other people's experiments, and this should come as a bonus on reading the book. However, this book is addressed directly to the readers who want to experiment but do not know how to go about it, and my interest and sympathies lie with them and their problems. If you already have a specific problem that you would like to turn into an experiment, well and good. It will not be a bad thing for you to go through, trying each thing in turn to see whether it fits in with your problem. If you do not have a problem, no need to worry. Providing you keep your eyes and ears open you will be assailed at each and every turn by problems that could make interesting experiments. If, by the time you have reached the end of the book, you are just as keen but still without a problem, the last chapter suggests some of the things that you might do about it.

What is an experiment anyway?

In an experiment, one investigates the relationship between two things by deliberately producing a change in one of them and looking at, observing, the change in the other. These 'things' in which change takes place are usually called **variables**.

The variable which we, as experimenters, are directly manipulating is called the **independent variable**. The variable in which we are looking for any consequent changes is called the **dependent variable**.

To take an example: suppose that one is interested in the effects of lack of sleep on the performance of some complex task. An experiment could be devised where the independent variable would be the number of hours without sleep, and the dependent variable some measure of the performance of the task, for example, the number of errors made.

Doing experiments, then, is a special form of observation – of controlled observation. One can see its special features by comparing experimentation with natural observation, or with the survey and the case study, which are other kinds of observation. In all these latter cases one simply looks at what is happening or has happened, without deliberately producing changes. A basic difference between the experiment and these other forms is that the experiment, in deliberately manipulating one variable, aims at controlling all other variables so that they do not affect the outcome.

To take an example once again: suppose that the problem is concerned with the relative effectiveness of lectures given in the early morning or late afternoon. In this case the independent variable is the time of the lectures, and the dependent variable some measure of the effectiveness of the lectures. This measure might, for instance, be the amount of information remembered after the lectures. Now there are many other things which might affect the amount remembered, apart from the time of the lecture – the students might be different, or the lecturer, or the material of the lecture, or the lecture room, or the conditions in the room, or what happened in the hour before the lecture – and one could go on and on. What we are saying here is that there are other variables, apart from the independent variable, which might affect the dependent variable. Providing the experimenter has sufficient patience, cunning and ingenuity, he or she can arrange to control all these other variables in such a way that they will not affect the assessment of the relationship between the independent and dependent variables.

The experiment is by no means limited to a consideration of a single, independent variable and its possible effects on a single dependent variable. Most published experiments involve the manipulation of several independent variables and there is a trend towards studies with more than one dependent variable. However such studies, to be adequately analysed, tend to involve complex statistical techniques which are beyond the range of the introductory text.

In natural observation, all variables are free to vary. Because of this, inferences which we make from natural observations and other non-experimental methods suffer from a serious defect. We can never be sure that changes in one particular variable occur as a result of changes in a second particular variable. In other words, from natural observation we can make no definite statements about causal relationships between variables. It is always possible that a third variable is causally related to both of the first two and has produced the relationship observed between them. For instance, natural observation would demonstrate a relationship between the softness of tar and the number of guardsmen fainting on parade.

Any direct causal relationship, such as the poor chaps being over-come by noxious fumes from the tar, appears to be highly unlikely, and I would surmise (although I have not tested this) that an actual experiment would fail to demonstrate any relationship. The obvious causal link is, of course, that of temperature – the rising tempera-ture causes both the tar to soften and the guardsmen to faint.

A more serious example is the relationship, found by several surveys, between smoking and lung cancer. Although actual experi-ments with animals have demonstrated a direct relationship, these experiments have not, for obvious reasons, been extended to human beings. Hence it is possible that, although there is a strong relationship between smoking and cancer, smoking may not be the cause of cancer. The cause may be in some personality or other psychological characteristics which predispose to both smoking and cancer.

This is not to say that natural observation has no part in investiga-tions, psychological or otherwise. There are many situations where direct experimentation is not possible. Perfectly respectable scien-ces such as astronomy and geology have to rely almost exclusively on natural observation. There are ethical reasons why variables involving painful stimuli, surgical operations and so on, may not be manipulated, and here natural observation is the only possibility.

There are also strong arguments for conducting at least the initial stages of investigation into an area by natural observation, even when experimentation is feasible. In this way it is possible to get some idea of which variables are most important. It may well be the case that variables which have marked effects under experimental conditions would be completely overshadowed by other variables under natural conditions.

This is not to suggest that there is a necessary connection between doing experiments and working in laboratories. It has been stressed that the central feature of the experiment is the deliberate mani-pulation of some variable and the ingenuous experimenter may well find ways of setting this up in the market, street, pub or wherever. Some lack of control over variables is probably inevitable but the increased naturalness of the setting may well reap considerable benefits.

A warning

Finally, a warning against over-optimism and against the rejection of non-experimental wisdom. There was a wave of enthusiasm for experimentation in education in the 1920s. This was followed by a wave of pessimism and disillusionment. The advocates of experimentation assumed that progress in teaching methods had been slow just because scientific method had not been applied. When the experiments proved to be tedious, equivocal, difficult to replicate and to accord with common sense, then disillusionment and rejection of experimentation took place. The justification for the experimental method does not lie in the fact that it is a panacea, but that it is the best method we know for getting at cause-and-effect relationships.

2 An experiment

Do you have a problem?

You may have problems or questions of your own which you would like to turn into actual experiments. If so, good. What I am going to do now is to go through the steps you might take in transforming the probably vague, ill-formulated idea for an experiment into an actual, concrete experimental design.

Suppose one is interested in absent-mindedness; a topic which is familiar enough but which has, until recently, been largely neglected by the psychologist. The interested reader is referred to Baddeley (1981) who discusses work which he and others have done in this area as examples of studies of the cognitive psychology of everyday life.

The first step in designing an experiment is to try to get a reasonably explicit statement of the problem with which one is trying to deal. What is meant by absent-mindedness? It appears to be connected with not remembering to do something. I am reminded in this connection of a former colleague who would probably win prizes for absent-mindedness. While this showed itself in a variety of ways his particular speciality lay in keys and cheque-books which were regularly mislaid. That is he would forget to bring his keys with him when leaving the house or he would leave his cheque-book on the desk after using it, where it would be obliterated by papers. This was not a case of someone poor at either remembering or recall of material in the usual sense; certainly he had an almost encyclopaedic knowledge of the published research in his area of specialism. What might well be involved here is the problem of giving himself a cue to check something at a particular time. Is his difficulty that of checking that he has his key when leaving the house?

Clearly one could move from the anecdotal to design an experiment where one or more aspects of remembering to check something at a particular time are tested. This is the approach taken by Baddeley and his colleagues in a variety of tasks including having people return postcards to them at specified dates after they had been given them, and a simulation of the pill-taking regime of 'four times a day after meals' where volunteers had to press a button on a modified watch at four specified times each day.

However there may be other facets of absent-mindedness as exemplified by going to a local café for a cup of tea and asking for a newspaper, as I did a few weeks ago. This aspect was investigated by a group of students from Bexhill Sixth Form College in connection with the 1980 B.B.C. television series 'Young Scientist of the Year' (further details are given in Baddeley, 1981). Their initial investigations of such 'slips of action' (other examples being answering the telephone by giving an address and trying to put on tights while wearing slippers) showed that there were quite considerable differences between individuals in the extent to which they reported such things as happening to them, and that the slips tended to occur when trying to perform a routine activity at the same time as doing something else.

The strategy of the Bexhill sixth-formers was to isolate two 'extreme' groups of people; one group who reported that they had no slips of this kind, and a second group who reported a lot of such slips. These two groups were then subjected to experimental situations where they had to perform two tasks at the same time.

We will consider further details in a little while, but for the moment let us discuss some of the technical language used to describe experiments.

Independent and dependent variables

The terms 'independent variable' and 'dependent variable' were introduced on p. 19 when we were discussing what we meant by an experiment. However, it will not do any harm to go through this again. What we are doing in our experiment is trying to observe the relationship between two variables.

The variable which the experimenter manipulates is called the **independent variable (IV)**. The IV here is 'absent-mindedness'. You should note that, as in many psychological experiments, the variable is being manipulated by the way in which the experimenter selects the groups and not by a direct manipulation of the degree to which a particular subject is absent-minded. A similar example occurs in experiments looking at sex differences where the experimenter selects female and male groups. There are, however, many situations where it is perfectly feasible to manipulate the independent variable directly by, for example, altering the type of material presented or in some other way changing the type of experience or situation for different groups.

The variable which is observed in order to see whether changes in the IV have any effect on it is known as the **dependent variable (DV)**. Here the DV is the performance of the task. Strictly speaking we can consider the performance of the two tasks which are carried out in the experiment as constituting two separate dependent variables.

In psychological experiments the independent variable is almost always either concerned with a property of the people taking part in the experiment (e.g. 'male' or 'female') or a stimulus variable (e.g. type of material to be learned, brightness of a light, exposure-time of a word, etc.): that is, in general, the **input** to the organism. Conversely, the dependent variable is almost always a response variable (time taken to make a response, strength of response, number of responses, etc.): that is, in general, the **output** from the organism.

Qualitative and quantitative variables

Fairly obviously, a 'variable' is something which can vary. In other words, it can take on different values or levels. For instance, if the variable is the number of errors made (a dependent variable) this might take on just about any whole-number (integral) value. In an experiment where we are considering how problem-solving varies with age, the independent variable would be age, and the values (or levels) of the variable used might be 4 years, 6 years, 8 years, 10 years, etc. There will be occasions when the independent variable is not quantitative in this way. In our 'absent-mindedness' example the independent variable is in fact 'absent-mindedness'. The two values of this variable, 'high absent-mindedness' and 'low absent-mindedness', while they are derived from numerical values are in fact treated qualitatively rather than quantitatively.

Experimental conditions

The values of the IV ('all-digit' and 'old-type') are usually called the **experimental conditions**. In this experiment, and in almost all the other experiments considered in this book, we will deal with just two values of the IV (i.e. two experimental conditions). This is partly because the statistical techniques that will be covered can only deal with two conditions at a time. However, keeping within these limits, it is possible to answer a very large number of experimental problems. There are, of course, techniques for dealing with more than two conditions at a time, and these are covered in more advanced texts. The other possibility is to deal with more complicated experimental designs by considering the values of the independent variable two at a time.

Operational definitions

An **operational definition** is stated in terms of the steps or operations that have to be carried out in observing or measuring whatever it is that is being defined. Before we can make the idea for the experiment into an actual concrete experiment, we must define our independent and dependent variables in this way.

Thus in considering the independent variable, what exactly do we mean by 'low absent-mindedness' and 'high absent-mindedness'? Here the procedure was to ask for recording of the absent-minded 'slips' over a four-week period; those reporting no instances over the period were assigned to the 'low absent-mindedness' group; those reporting more than eight to the 'high absent-mindedness' group.

As far as the dependent variable is concerned it is necessary to specify the exact nature of the two tasks and exactly what we will measure. The two tasks were backward counting in threes from a specified number and mirror-drawing. The latter, if you are not familiar with it, is a common laboratory task involving tracing around the outline of a star with the tracing hand only visible through a mirror. The measure in the first task was the number of items counted in a specified time and in the second task the time taken to complete the maze.

It is only when we have precisely defined the variables that the experiment can be carried out. Equally important, it is essential that we define the terms in this way so that some later worker, coming along and seeing our results, being interested in them or perhaps even disbelieving them, will then be able to set up an exact replica of our experiment in order to check on the result we have obtained.

This is called **replication** of the experiment, and Baddeley notes with regret that the particular findings of the 'Bexhill' study have, to date, proved impossible to replicate. Perhaps we can leave further studies in this area as a challenge to the reader.

Subjects, samples and populations

The people or animals who undergo an experiment are referred to as **subjects**. The symbol S is used to indicate a subject (but it is sometimes used in statistics to stand for other things – so beware).

We now have some important decisions to make as to *what* kind of subjects, which leads us on to a discussion of samples and populations.

When we gather results from subjects in an experiment we do not usually want our results to be applicable only to the subjects we have used. We would like to be able to generalize rather more widely than this. If we draw our subjects in an unbiased way as a sample from some particular population, then it is possible for the results to be generalized from the sample to the population as a whole. A sample which is unbiased, in the sense that each member of the population has got an equal chance of appearing in the sample, is known as a **random sample**. This idea is central to much of the statistical reasoning developed later in the book and will be returned to.

It is often the case that the subjects for an experiment come from a captive audience (e.g. the members of a class in practical psychology). In this case one cannot reasonably think of the subjects as forming a sample from any (obvious) population.

The three basic designs or how do *S*s fit into the experiment?

Given that we have chosen our IV and DV and decided on the way in which they will be operationally defined in the experimental situation, some of the most important decisions remaining relate to the way in which *S*s are assigned to the different conditions.

These ways of assignment lead to three basic experimental designs:

independent *S*s,
matched *S*s,
repeated measures.

1 The independent-subjects design

For this design a group of subjects is obtained for the experiment as a whole, and then individuals are allocated randomly to one or other of the experimental conditions. Thus if we decide to use sixteen subjects in all, they will be allocated randomly to the two conditions, with the single constraint that there will be equal numbers in the two groups. This could be done using a coin with heads for condition A say, and tails for condition B, or, alternatively, using odds and evens from random number tables. We would continue allocating in this way until eight subjects had been allocated to one of the two groups, when the remaining subjects would be allocated to the other group.

The allocation might be as follows:

Table 1 Allocation of subjects in
independent-subjects design

A	B
S1	S3
S2	S6
S4	S7
S5	S8
S9	S10
S12	S11
S13	S15
S14	S16

Here $S1$ stands for subject one, $S2$ for subject two, etc.

In the experiment each subject will provide us with a single score for purposes of analysis, i.e. the total number of subjects is the same as the total number of scores.

2 The matched-subjects design

In this design, subjects are matched in pairs and the members of the pairs allocated randomly, one to each of the experimental conditions. Any experimenter having access to pairs of identical twins would be addicted to this design, but there are other ways in which pairs can be obtained. The matching can be performed in terms of a third variable which the experimenter believes is likely to affect scores on the dependent variable. Thus in a problem-solving task, it would be possible to match subjects in terms of intelligence. If IQ test scores are available, pairs of subjects could be selected who were closely equated in terms of their scores. In the 'absent-mindedness' experiment it might, for instance, have been feasible to match subjects in terms of their performance on some memory task, e.g. in terms of their memory span.

The allocation might be as follows:

Table 2 Allocation of subjects
in matched-subjects design

A	B
S12	S11
S21	S22
S31	S32
S42	S41
S51	S52
S62	S61
S71	S72
S82	S81

Here $S11$ stands for subject 1 in the first matched pair and $S12$ stands for subject 2 in the first matched pair. $S21$ stands for subject 1 in the second matched pair, and so on. The decision about whether 1 or 2 within each pair is allocated to condition A or B is on a random basis.

As with the independent-subjects design, each subject will provide us with a single score for analysis, the total number of subjects again being the same as the total number of scores.

3 The repeated-measures design

In this design, a single subject appears under both of the experimental conditions. Thus for the same number of scores as the other two designs we need half the number of subjects.

Table 3 Allocation of subjects
in repeated-measures design

A	B
S1	S1
S2	S2
S3	S3
S4	S4
S5	S5
S6	S6
S7	S7
S8	S8

Here $S1$ stands for the same subject under both experimental conditions, $S2$ stands for a second subject, who also appears under both conditions, and so on.

Although there are obviously no problems here in terms of the allocation of subjects to the different experimental conditions, there are special problems relating to the order in which each subject performs under the two experimental conditions. These problems are referred to (pp. 32–3) under the headings of Counterbalancing and Randomization.

The single-subject design

In some situations, considerations of economy (both of time and of trouble) point to the use of just one subject in an experiment. Whilst this design appears attractive and has a long history in psychology – Ebbinghaus in the nineteenth century performed a monumental series of single-subject experiments using himself as his only subject – it has considerable difficulties. It has been mentioned that, in a repeated-measures design, complexities arise due to order and similar effects. In a single-subject design we have a whole series of repeated measures, and any one measure may be dependent in subtle and complex ways on the measures previously taken. If we have a situation where it is known that the successive scores obtained from a subject are independent of each other, then there is no statistical objection to single-subject designs. This could be, for instance, in a simple motor task where no knowledge of results is given. Indeed a strong case can be made out that psychology is, or should be, concerned with the behaviour of the individual organism and that, by taking group data, we obscure the phenomena in which we are interested. However it is undeniably true that the human being is a learning animal, that experiences *do* modify behaviour in many ways, and hence that in general there will be various dependencies between successive measures taken in a single-subject design. As we shall see, many of the statistical tests rest on the assumption that scores are independent and hence we must say, somewhat regretfully, that they cannot be used appropriately with single-subject designs unless we can persuade ourselves that we have independent scores.

An experiment

A somewhat different approach concentrating on the analysis of results from single-subjects has been advocated by B. F. Skinner. This depends on demonstrating effects within the individual subject as changes from a steady 'base-line'. Skinner argues that, using his techniques, it should be possible to exert such a degree of control over extraneous variables that the effect of changes in the independent variable becomes so clear and obvious that statistical analysis is unnecessary. His approach has many followers in both pure and applied psychology. A clear exposition of this alternative methodology is given in Sidman (1960).

Experimental and other effects

The change in the DV produced by the change in IV is called an **experimental effect**. However, there may well be changes in the DV produced by variables other than the IV.

Let us take as an example a very common effect in psychological experimentation. Suppose that in an experiment we have decided to use a repeated-measures design. Now if each subject were to be tested with condition A first and then condition B afterwards the **experimental effect** is *confounded* by a possible **order** effect. Thus it might be that in this situation there is a general practice effect (increased familiarity with the situation, 'learning how to learn', etc.) such that whatever is done second gets the higher score. Alternatively, it might be that there is a negative practice effect of a general kind (fatigue, boredom, etc.) such that whatever is done second gets the lower score.

In either case we cannot make unambiguous statements about the experimental effect, i.e. as to whether condition A or condition B produces the better results, because what we actually measure is the combination of the experimental effect and the order effect.

Counterbalancing

One method which is often used in an attempt to overcome the order effect and similar effects is to **counterbalance** the order of presentation of the different experimental conditions to the subjects. This means that in our example when a repeated-measures design is used, half of the subjects work under condition A first, and half work under condition B first.

Table 4 Counterbalancing subjects

A	B
S1 (first)	S1 (second)
S2 (second)	S2 (first)
S3 (first)	S3 (second)
S4 (second)	S4 (first)
S5 (first)	S5 (second)
S6 (second)	S6 (first)
S7 (first)	S7 (second)
S8 (second)	S8 (first)

Counterbalancing will balance out an order effect only if this effect is of the straightforward kind mentioned above, where the order effect is, say, adding a constant amount to the score of whatever comes second. It is quite possible that the order effect is more complicated – that for instance there is a large order effect when condition A comes first, and only a small order effect when condition B comes first. This kind of effect is called an **interaction** and, if it occurs, counterbalancing will only partially balance out the order effect. Notice that in neither case can we get rid of the order effect and that, even when it is a simple additive type, the order effect, whilst not biasing the result, will tend to obscure the experimental effect that we are interested in.

Randomization

An alternative to counterbalancing is **randomization**. This means we could decide, by tossing a coin separately for each subject, whether he or she does condition A or condition B first. A fuller discussion of randomization and its relation to statistical inference follows in the next chapter. There are suggestions for methods of randomization in different situations in Appendix 1 (p. 152).

The steps to be taken in designing an experiment are taken up again in Chapter 8, after the various statistical techniques have been discussed in the intervening chapters.

3 Statistical inference

Constant and random errors

In our experiment, we are trying to find the effect, if any, that the independent variable has on the dependent variable. As discussed in the last chapter, the dependent variable may be affected by variables other than the independent variable. These other confounding variables may produce two kinds of errors – **random** errors and **constant** errors.

For example, in experiments with animals, food is often used as a reward for food-deprived animals. The method commonly used at one time to ensure that they were appropriately food-deprived was to allow access to food for only a short time, say thirty minutes, per day. However, different animals would take in different amounts of food during this time. If performance in some task were related to food deprivation, then there would be variations in performance which would contribute random errors to any experiment using this method of food deprivation.

A constant error would occur if, for some reason, all the animals in one experimental condition were able to eat for longer than those in another condition. Hence the direction of the error would always be the same – i.e. constant.

Notice that random and constant errors have different effects: a random error obscures the experimental effect we are interested in, a constant error biases or distorts the results.

Constant errors must go!

Our business in designing an experiment is to hunt down all possible sources of constant error. In some cases it is possible to eliminate them completely by means of direct control. A constant error would be introduced in comparing heights of eskimo and pygmy children if a ruler were used which expanded as the temperature increased; this could be controlled and completely eliminated by using a non-expanding ruler. (Incidentally, this is not put forward as a useful tip, it is simply intended as a clear example.) In other cases one may not be able to control directly, but the biasing effect can be removed either by counterbalancing (as in the case of simple order effects) or, more generally, by randomization. However, neither counter-balancing nor randomization eliminates the error; they merely have the effect of transforming it from constant error to random error. This means that they remove the error as a source of bias, but it still remains to obscure the experimental effect in which we are in-terested. Whilst it may appear desirable to eliminate all possible constant errors by direct control, there are arguments in favour of not doing this.

Consider what might be called the 'left-handed, fifty-three-year-old introverted Isle of Wight rat-catcher' experiment. In setting up this particular hypothetical experiment it might appear likely that the handedness of the subjects would be related to their perform-ance. Using direct control we would decide to work either entirely with left-handers, or entirely with right-handers – say the former. Similarly, age could be seen as a possible variable, and using direct control we would opt for a particular age or age range for our subjects. In like manner, personality variables, geographical loca-tion and profession might also be seen as having a potential effect in our experiment. Clearly the end result is ludicrous. Not only is it highly unlikely that we would be able to find even a single individual to fit the bill, let alone a viable group to carry out the experiment, but even if by some miracle this were possible the generality of any results we obtained would be highly questionable.

Put in more general terms it may well be that experimental effects can be demonstrated when everything in sight is held constant. It may possibly happen that this effect is dependent on the particular values of one or more of the variables held constant. If we had, by chance, held them constant at a different value, then the ex-perimental effect might have disappeared. The alternative to direct control is randomization, and if the experimental effect still stands when these variables have been randomized, it indicates that the effect is reasonably robust.

Random errors will not go!

Some random errors can be eliminated as, for example, those caused by the animals eating different amounts during their thirty-minute feeding period. A better method, now widely used, is to feed the animals a carefully measured amount of food which maintains them at a given percentage of their free-feeding body weight. Thus, if we can assume that the effect of food deprivation is directly dependent on this percentage, the random error attributable to differences in food deprivation can be completely eliminated.

However, there are many random errors which cannot be eliminated in this way. Consider the many things which might affect a human subject's performance on a memory or a learning task. In order to control these effects one would need a set of subjects with identical heredity and environment. Their learning and other experiences before the experiment would have to be equated. They would need to be of the same intelligence and have the same personality and attitudes, to be in the same state of health, etc., etc. The list is endless, and it would be impossible to contemplate even starting any experiments if this kind of control were a necessary prerequisite.

What we do of course is to choose our subjects, where possible, at random from the population we are interested in, and we make sure that the allocation to the different experimental conditions is random so that any potential constant errors end up as random errors.

One is forced to conclude that random error is here to stay and that our methods will have to take this into account.

Statistical inference and probability

Granted, then, that random error will be present, both in its own right and as a result of our having randomized constant errors, how can it be disentangled from the experimental effect that we are after? The answer is that we make use of statistical inference.

What we do is:

1 *Estimate how probable it is that the random error by itself could produce the changes in the dependent variable observed in the experiment.*

If

2 *It seems unlikely that random error by itself could produce these changes*

then

3 *We decide that it is the independent variable which is having an effect on the dependent variable.*

You should read through these points several times. The idea is very important and the process is the reverse of what many people expect, i.e. we come to a decision about the independent variable's effect not directly, but by discounting the likelihood that the effect was produced by random error.

As you will see, what is done is to use statistics to make inferences about these effects – hence 'statistical inference'. Let us make a start on this by considering the concept of 'probability'.

Probability

The concept of probability is controversial among both statisticians and philosophers. It is used in at least three different ways. In everyday life the reference is usually to how likely or unlikely it is that a future event will occur. Thus we have statements such as 'Huddersfield Town will probably win on Saturday' or 'You'll probably be sick if you eat that third cream cake'. Sometimes this feeling of doubt or uncertainty is expressed in numerical terms as 'I think it's 10 to 1 against that he will stop smoking before Christmas' but even so these are subjective estimates and as such this use of the term is commonly referred to as **subjective probability**.

A second use of the term derives from analyses of card games and other games of chance. In cutting a well-shuffled pack of playing cards what is the probability that the card turned over is an ace? This approach defines probability as the **ratio of the number of favourable cases** (here the four aces) to the **total number of equally likely cases** (here the fifty-two cards, assuming a normal pack with no jokers). The probability is then 1 in 13 or 1/13. This idea, and particularly the notion of 'equally likely cases', enables one to work out theoretically the probability of various events occurring in quite complex situations and is of considerable value to casino owners and the like. You should note however that this is a formal, theoretical approach to probability sometimes referred to as **mathematical probability**, and the extent to which it corresponds to real life in any situation depends on whether the theoretical assumptions (and in particular the idea of equally likely cases) apply in that particular situation. When playing with dice it seems reasonable to assume that each of the six alternatives resulting from rolling a single dice is equally likely. However such things as loaded dice are not unknown and if over a period we find in practice that, say, a 1 comes up on over half the rolls, then the applicability of the theory in this case is cast into considerable doubt.

This last example illustrates a third approach to probability, the so-called 'relative frequency' approach, otherwise known as **empirical probability**. Here the probability of an event is estimated by the *ratio of the number of times the event occurs to the total number of trials which have taken place*. It is an estimate because the actual number of trials which have taken place are regarded as a sample from the infinitely large population of trials which could theoretically take place. The probability is the state of affairs in this population and will tend to be more and more accurately estimated as we increase the size of the sample. Anyone with a few days to spare might like to test this by tossing a coin repeatedly and noting the proportion of heads obtained after, say, ten trials, a hundred trials, a thousand trials, etc.

These three approaches to probability are not necessarily incompatible. In particular the mathematical and empirical approaches often helpfully complement each other. The mathematical approach to coin tossing obviously gives a probability of a half for heads and various lengthy series of coin tosses which have been carried out give estimates, as one might expect subjectively, that are essentially the same.

Expressed numerically, probability (for which the symbol p is normally used) has a minimum value of 0 and a maximum value of 1, where 0 refers to something which never occurs and 1 to something which always occurs. In practice, of course, most of the things in which we are interested have probability values between these extremes.

Consider an experiment. Suppose that in a repeated-measures design we found seven out of eight scores better with condition A than with condition B, and only one out of eight better with condition B. What is the probability that we would have obtained that result on a chance basis, i.e. if only random effects are involved and there is no effect due to experimental conditions?

Let us refer to the case when condition A scores are higher than condition B as $+$, and when they score lower as $-$. Using mathematical probability we can take the assumption that only random effects are involved as equivalent to the assumption of equally likely outcomes. That is, the probability of getting a $+$ is $\frac{1}{2}$, and also the probability of getting a $-$ is $\frac{1}{2}$ (if you find it easier, think in terms of the probability of getting 'heads' when you toss a coin).

Suppose we consider two subjects together. There are then three possibilities: two $+$s, one $+$ and zero $+$s. What are the probabilities associated with these? A 'family tree' helps to demonstrate this (Figure 1).

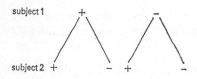

Figure 1 'Family tree' for two subjects

There is a total of four possible outcomes which we can again assume to be equally likely: first, subject 1 getting $+$ and subject 2 getting $+$; second, subject 1 getting $+$ and subject 2 getting $-$; third, subject 1 getting $-$ and subject 2 getting $+$; fourth, subject 1 getting $-$ and subject 2 getting $-$. Considering these four possible outcomes two $+$s occurs once in four (i.e. $p = \frac{1}{4} = 0 \cdot 25$), one $+$ occurs twice in four (i.e. $p = \frac{2}{4} = 0 \cdot 5$) and zero $+$s occurs once in four (i.e. $p = \frac{1}{4} = 0 \cdot 25$).

In this way it is possible to work out the probability, on a chance basis, of getting any given number of $+$s from any number of subjects. For four subjects, the 'family tree' looks like Figure 2.

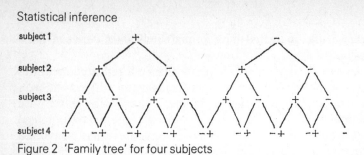

Figure 2 'Family tree' for four subjects

There is a total of sixteen possible outcomes and a table of probabilities can be obtained as shown in Table 5.

Table 5 Probabilities for different numbers of +s with four subjects

Number of +s	Probability (= fraction of outcomes)
4	$\frac{1}{16} = 0.0625$
3	$\frac{4}{16} = 0.2500$
2	$\frac{6}{16} = 0.3750$
1	$\frac{4}{16} = 0.2500$
0	$\frac{1}{16} = 0.0625$

Moving on to our example of eight subjects, the drawing of the family tree is left to the reader, the total number of possible outcomes now being 256. The table of probabilities is given in Table 6.

Table 6 Probabilities for different numbers of +s with eight subjects

Number of +s	Probability (= fraction of outcomes)
8	$\frac{1}{256} = 0.004$
7	$\frac{8}{256} = 0.031$
6	$\frac{28}{256} = 0.110$
5	$\frac{56}{256} = 0.220$
4	$\frac{70}{256} = 0.270$
3	$\frac{56}{256} = 0.220$
2	$\frac{28}{256} = 0.110$
1	$\frac{8}{256} = 0.031$
0	$\frac{1}{256} = 0.004$

We can see from the table that the probability of obtaining seven +s out of eight is 0·031.

But how does this relate to our analysis of the experiment? This can be shown in graphical form in what is called a histogram or bar-chart. A bar is drawn for each number of +s, the height of the bar representing the probability in each case (Figure 3).

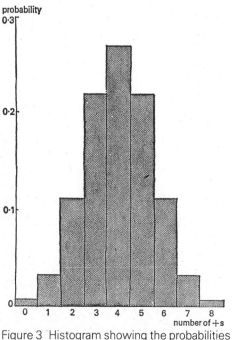

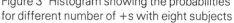

Figure 3 Histogram showing the probabilities for different number of +s with eight subjects

Significance level

As stated before, we decide that the independent variable has affected the dependent variable when the probability of getting the result obtained, if random errors only are involved, is sufficiently low.

The histogram shown above gives the distribution of the number of +s out of eight when it is pure chance whether or not any particular result ends up as + or −. If we were to consider the extremes of this distribution, the probability of getting no +s at all is 0·004, i.e. very low. Similarly the probability of getting all +s is 0·004. We might feel that these probabilities are so low that we are justified in rejecting the hypothesis that the results obtained are due to random errors alone. How low does the probability have to be before we reject this hypothesis? There is no definitive answer to the question; whatever level we choose, it is possible to make an error. In fact, there are two possible kinds of error. What is usually called a **type 1 error** occurs when we decide that the independent variable had an effect on the dependent variable when it did not have (i.e. when, in fact, the change in the dependent variable was due to the random effects alone).

A **type 2 error** occurs when we conclude that the independent variable had no effect on the dependent variable when, in fact, there was a genuine relationship.

What is normally done is to choose a **significance level**. The significance level is simply the probability of making a type 1 error. The meaning of significance level is quite often misunderstood, and it will perhaps be useful to talk around this a little more.

Refer back to Figure 3. Suppose that we set a significance level of $p = 0·008$, then, with a result of 8 +s or of 0 +s, we would come to the decision that the IV had an effect on the DV, i.e. that the result was sufficiently improbable for us to decide that it was not due to random errors alone. Note, by the way, that the significance level of $p = 0·008$ was chosen to make life easy, as the probability of 8 +s and that of 0 +s adds up to 0·008.

Suppose that we are willing to take a somewhat higher risk of making a type 1 error, say $p = 0·070$ (again carefully chosen to make life easy). You should then be able to see that with results of 8, 7, 1 or 0 +s we would decide that the IV had an effect on the DV. Notice here that, if you are going to say that with 7 +s the decision is that the IV has an effect, you obviously must also say this for 8 +s, i.e. for any more extreme result.

The lower the probability set for the significance level – and hence the less chance of making a type 1 error – the greater the chance of making a type 2 error. In other words, by limiting your decision that the IV affects the DV to the very extreme cases, you are making it more likely that in some cases you will decide incorrectly that there wasn't any effect. So some kind of balance has to be struck between these two errors.

There is a convention whereby a significance level of probability $p = 0.05$ (the 5 per cent significance level) is referred to as **significant** and the significance level of probability $p = 0.01$ (the 1 per cent significance level) is referred to as **highly significant**. However there is nothing magic about these particular figures. It may be (for example, in exploratory research into an area) that one is worried about type 2 errors, i.e. about regarding as non-significant a relationship which perhaps ought to be followed up, and hence that a significance level of $p = 0.10$ might be preferable. On the other hand, there are situations where the consequences of making a type 1 error might be particularly worrying (owing, perhaps, to one's theories being at variance with other published work), and a significance level of $p = 0.001$ might be indicated.

If we decide, however, to be conventional and to use, say, a 5 per cent ($p = 0.05$) significance level, what decision do we come to in our experiment? Referring back to the histogram showing the distribution of +s (Figure 3), the significance level is used to divide the dependent variable into two regions – a region where we will decide that random effects alone are involved, and one where we will decide that the independent variable did have an effect on the dependent variable. A glance at Table 6 (p. 40) reveals that, if the cut-off points are marked as shown in Figure 4, the total probability of making a type 1 error is $p = 0.008$.

If the cut-off point had been moved in to include the 1 + and 7 + cases, the total probability of making a type 1 error increases to $p = 0.070$. This latter value would exceed the significance level, which we had set at $p = 0.05$ – i.e. too much of the distribution is being cut off and the cut-off points actually shown on the diagram should be used. As our observed number of +s in the experiment was 7, we see that this lies in the region 'decide IV had no effect on DV', and hence we cannot regard this as evidence for a relationship between independent variable and dependent variable.

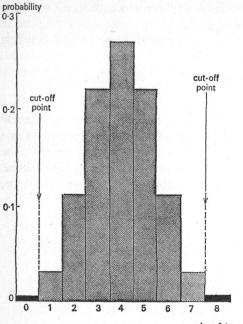

Figure 4 Histogram from Figure 3 with cut-off points added

Hypotheses and Hypothesis Testing

You will often find issues about whether or not the IV affects the DV referred to in terms of the **null hypothesis** (H_0) and the **alternative hypothesis** (H_1). In this language, the null hypothesis is that the IV does not affect the DV. Various alternative hypotheses are possible, but the most general one would be that the IV does affect the DV.

When the experiment and analysis are completed we then
either reject H_0 and accept H_1, if the result is less probable than the chosen significance level,

or 'accept' H_0 and reject H_1 if the result is more probable than the chosen significance level.

Some statisticians consider it inappropriate to talk about 'accepting' H_0 and prefer 'fail to reject' H_0 instead. This is because in 'accepting' H_0 we don't mean that it is likely that H_0 is true, only that we don't have evidence to reject it.

The sign test

It is perfectly possible to work out the probabilities of different outcomes for any number of pluses and minuses, but this can become somewhat laborious – particularly for large samples. The information from computations like this is incorporated in Table B p. 163), which can be used as shown below to determine the statistical significance of one's results.

Step-by-step procedure

Sign test

Use this test when you have pairs of scores (i.e. matched-subjects or repeated-measures designs)

Step 1 Give each pair of scores a plus $(+)$ if the score in the left-hand condition exceeds that in the right-hand condition, a minus $(-)$ if the score in the left-hand condition is less than that in the right-hand condition, a zero (0) if there is no difference.

Step 2 Note the number of times (L) the less frequent sign occurs and the total number (T) of pluses and minuses. *Ignore all zeros*, i.e. do not include them in T.

Step 3 Look up in Table B (p. 163) the highest value of L which is significant at the 5% level for this value of T.

Step 4 If your value of L is equal to or lower than the value obtained from the table, the decision is made that the IV had an effect on the DV – the results are referred to as 'significant at the 5% level'. If your value of L is greater than the table value, then the decision is made that the independent variable had no effect on the dependent variable – the results are 'not significant'.

Step 5 Translate the result of the statistical test back in terms of the experiment.

Worked example

Sign test

The following scores were obtained in a matched-subjects design with nine pairs of subjects.

A	B	Step 1
12	7	+
10	8	+
15	11	+
8	8	0
7	8	−
10	9	+
8	4	+
7	5	+
13	9	+

Step 2 $L = 1$, $T = 8$

Step 3 From Table B, highest value of $L = 0$ for significance when $T = 8$.

Step 4 As our value of L is greater than this we decide that the IV has no effect on the DV – i.e. the results are not significant.

Step 5 The difference between condition A and condition B is not significant at the 5% level.

Note (a) The results obtained are identical to those obtained by a direct calculation of probabilities (p. 43).

(b) Although the results are not significant, there is a suggestion that there are higher scores under condition A; this should perhaps be explored in a more extensive experiment.

4 Descriptive statistics

What are descriptive statistics?

It is obvious that the results of an experiment should be displayed in a form which makes them readily comprehensible to the reader. This can be done by drawing up clear tables of results and by grouping these results together in various ways, as appropriate. The same information can often be displayed to advantage by the use of a graphical method, e.g. by a histogram, as was done in the last chapter when probabilities of different numbers of pluses were plotted.

A second way of presenting the results to the reader so that they can easily be understood is in terms of **descriptive statistics** which summarize certain aspects of the results. Two types of descriptive statistics are commonly used – ones which give a measure of **central tendency** (what one might call the *most typical value*) and ones which give a measure of **dispersion** (the *variability* or '*spread*') for a set of results. These statistics are measures which we compute from the sample of scores we have collected. Very often we use the statistic as an estimate of the state of affairs in the population.

Measures of central tendency

1 The arithmetic mean

This is a commonly used measure of *most typical value*. It is the average of a set of scores, obtained by adding all scores together and dividing by the number of scores. This provides us with a simple example of the use of symbols. Let the scores in general be represented by the symbol X: the first score by X_1, the second by X_2, right through to the last of a total of N scores, which is represented by X_N. If we represent the mean score by the symbol $\overline{X}$, usually referred to as 'X bar', then

$$\overline{X} = \frac{\text{total of all scores}}{\text{total number of scores}}$$

$$= \frac{X_1 + X_2 + X_3 + \ldots + X_N}{N}.$$

This can alternatively be expressed as

$$\overline{X} = \frac{\Sigma X}{N},$$

where ΣX means the total of all the X scores.

For example, if the scores are:

7, 3, 11, 12, 9, 14,

then $\Sigma X = 7 + 3 + 11 + 12 + 9 + 14$,

$\qquad N = 6$,

and $\qquad \overline{X} = \frac{\Sigma X}{N} = \frac{56}{6} = 9 \cdot 3$,

i.e. the arithmetic mean is $9 \cdot 3$.

There are also geometric means and harmonic means, but these are used much less widely than the arithmetic mean and are not covered here.

2 The median

The median is a value chosen so that it has as many scores above it as it has below it. To obtain the median, the scores should be placed in order of size. If the total number of scores is odd, the median is then the central value; e.g. if there are eleven scores it is the sixth score from either end. If the total number of scores is even, then the median is conventionally taken as the arithmetic mean of the two central values. If the median falls within a cluster of scores which all have the same value, the simplest procedure is to give it that value.

(More complex methods for computing the median are often given, but the results seldom differ by an appreciable amount from the simple methods given here.)

As an example, if the scores are:

14, 9, 17, 21, 7, 18, 16, 22,

then, rearranging these in order of size:

7, 9, 14, 16, 17, 18, 21, 22.

There are eight scores, therefore the median is the average of the fourth and fifth scores:

$$\frac{16 + 17}{2} = 16 \cdot 5,$$

i.e. the median is 16·5.

3 Mode

The mode is the value *most frequently occurring* in a set of scores. It is often indeterminate when dealing with small sets of scores, but is commonly quoted for large samples. If a histogram is plotted, the peak of the histogram gives the modal value.

In some circumstances a histogram may show that there are two separated values which have frequencies greater than adjoining values. This is known as a *bimodal* distribution.

Figure 5 shows such an example, obtained when pigeons were rewarded with food for spacing their pecks at a key at least twenty seconds apart. A bimodal distribution often indicates that there are two separable sub-groups in the population. In this example we have one sub-group of 'spaced' pecks and one of short bursts of rapid pecks. The mode cannot be reasonably used as a measure of central tendency if there are two or more modal values.

Comparison of mean, median and mode

The arithmetic mean is the statistic most often used to give the typical value of a set of scores. Its advantage in theoretical terms is that it gives a better estimate of the population from which one

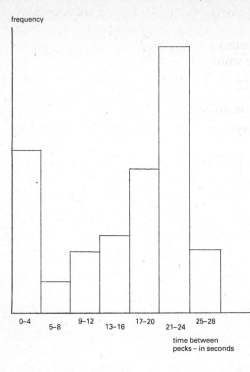

frequency

0–4 5–8 9–12 13–16 17–20 21–24 25–28

time between
pecks – in seconds

Figure 5 A bimodal distribution

sample of scores is drawn than the median, which is in turn better than the mode. The mean of a sample tends to differ less from the mean of the population than the median of the sample differs from the median of the population. This is because the mean extracts most information from the sample. One indication of this is that the mean would be altered by the alteration of any single one of the individual scores, i.e. the mean is dependent on the values of each of the scores in the sample.

In contrast, both the median and the mode may be unaffected by changing the value of a number of scores or, on the other hand, they may be greatly affected by changing the value of a small number of other scores.

51

Again in contrast to the mean, neither the median nor the mode is affected by extreme scores, either very high or very low. Thus, if the following scores represent time in seconds to solve some anagrams:

1, 2, 2, 3, 4, 5, 5, 6, 277,

an arithmetic mean would be unsuitable, as it would be dominated by the very high score produced by a subject with some type of block, whereas the median of 4 seconds gives a much better picture of the typical value.

Measures of dispersion

For the following scores:

17, 32, 34, 58, 69, 70, 98, 142,

the arithmetic mean is 65. The following set of scores also has a mean value of 65:

61, 62, 64, 65, 65, 66, 68, 69.

This suggests that the summary statistic of the mean above is insufficient. What is also needed is a statistic which gives an indication of the variability or spread in the data. Several such statistics have been devised, and five of them will now be mentioned.

1 Range

The range is simply the difference between the highest and lowest scores. The advantage of the range is that it is very simple to understand and very easy to compute. Thus all we do is arrange the scores in order of size.

For example:

19, 21, 22, 22, 25, 27, 28, 42.

The range is then the difference between highest and lowest scores, i.e. the **range** = 42 − 19 = 23.

The main disadvantage of the range is that it depends upon just the two extreme score values. If either or both of these differs by a large amount from the other scores, then the range will be greatly affected.

2 The semi-interquartile range

Measures of range other than the simple one mentioned above have sometimes been used. The most common of these is the semi-interquartile range. If the scores are arranged in ascending order of size, the point that cuts off the lowest $\frac{1}{4}$ or 25 per cent of the cases is called Q_1, the first quartile. The point that cuts off the lowest $\frac{3}{4}$ or 75 per cent of the cases is called Q_3, the third quartile. If, for instance, there are 24 scores, the first quartile Q_1 occurs between the 6th and 7th scores (take the average of these, as for the median). The third quartile Q_3 occurs between the 18th and 19th scores.

The interquartile range is the difference between the third and first quartiles and the semi-interquartile range is, fairly obviously, one half of this.

i.e. **semi-interquartile range** $= \dfrac{Q_3 - Q_1}{2}$

It may have occurred to you that what we have previously called the **median** could also be termed the **second quartile**.

The relative sizes of the differences $(Q_3 - Q_2)$ and $(Q_2 - Q_1)$ provides a useful measure of what is termed the **skewness** (or lack of symmetry) of the distribution of scores.

Thus Figure 6 shows three histograms, one with a longer tail to the left than to the right (called a negative skew), one symmetrical and one with a longer tail to the right than to the left (called a positive skew).

If negative skew, then $(Q_2 - Q_1) > (Q_3 - Q_2)$.
If positive skew, then $(Q_3 - Q_2) > (Q_2 - Q_1)$.

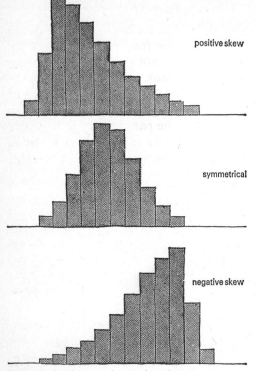

Figure 6 Positive and negative skew

The semi-interquartile range has an advantage over the range in that, whilst still relatively easy to compute, it makes use of more of the scores than the range. However, the values of the quartiles do not depend on the exact sizes of scores within the ranges chosen.

If the decision has been made to use the median as the measure of 'most typical value', then it generally follows that the semi-interquartile range would be used for the measure of variability.

3 Mean deviation

The deviation of a score from the mean is simply the difference between it and the mean. In symbols, if X is a score and $\overline{X}$ the mean score, then the deviation x is given by

$x = X - \overline{X}$.

The average of these deviations is no use as a measure of spread because it is inevitably zero. (This arises from the way in which the arithmetic mean is defined. If this is not clear to you from the algebra, take a set of figures and work out the average of the deviations from the mean.) Thus, for the mean deviation to be of any use, what is done is to ignore the sign of the difference, i.e. to call the deviation positive whether the particular score is greater than or less than the mean. This is known as the **absolute deviation** and is expressed as $|X - \overline{X}|$. Hence the mean deviation $\bar{x}$ becomes

$$\bar{x} = \frac{\Sigma |X - \overline{X}|}{N},$$

where N is the total number of scores and Σ means 'the sum of'. Compared with the range, the mean deviation has the advantage that it is based upon all of the scores and not just the highest and lowest. However, the mean deviation is, in fact, rarely used. It has been supplanted by another measure of variability based on deviations which will be considered now.

4 Variance

In considering the mean deviation, the point was made that, if signs are taken into account, the average deviation about the mean is always zero. The solution to this problem with the mean deviation was to ignore the signs of the differences. An alternative tactic is to take the squares of the deviations. This, of course, also has the effect of making the negative deviations positive (as 'negative times negative equals positive').

The mean squared deviation is a statistic which is commonly used and is called the variance. You would therefore expect the formula for the variance to be

$$\text{Variance} = \frac{\Sigma (X - \overline{X})^2}{N}$$

where X is the individual score,
$\overline{X}$ is the mean score,
N is the total number of scores,
Σ means 'the sum of'.

This formula is in fact used when we wish to measure the variance for the set of data that we actually have in front of us. This will either be when we have a sample and we simply wish to describe various aspects of that sample, or where by some prodigious feat we have managed to measure the whole of the population and in consequence know its mean exactly.

However, as has been stressed previously, we usually have a sample and are wanting to use that sample to make estimates about the population from which the sample is taken.

In these circumstances it can be shown (magic words) that an unbiased estimate of the variance is obtained by use of a slightly different formula,

$$\text{Variance} = \frac{\Sigma (X - \overline{X})^2}{N - 1}$$

The $N - 1$ in the denominator, which is substituted for the N in the previous formula, is referred to as the **degrees of freedom**. As the name suggests it is the number of deviations from the mean which are free to vary and is one less than the total N because when we know $N - 1$ of them the final deviation is fixed by the requirement that the overall mean deviation is zero. While I have to admit that this is not by any means an adequate explanation for the use of $N - 1$ in the formula, there is at least an intuitive rightness to the notion that our estimate of variation should be divided by the number of things that are free to vary.

5 Standard deviation

The variance is in squared units as compared with the original data. In many cases it is helpful to have the measure of variability in the same units as the original data and hence it seems appropriate to use the square root of the variance. This is given a special name, the **standard deviation (SD)**, i.e.

$$SD = \sqrt{\frac{\Sigma (X - \bar{X})^2}{N-1}}$$

This is by far the most commonly used of the measures of variability or spread. In practice a version of the formula, which looks somewhat different but is algebraically identical and which is somewhat easier to compute when using a calculator, is often substituted. This is

$$SD = \sqrt{\frac{\Sigma X^2 - (\Sigma X)^2/N}{(N-1)}}$$

where X is the individual score,

X^2 is the sum of the squared individual scores,

$(\Sigma X)^2$ is the sum of the individual scores which is then squared,

and N is the total number of scores.

You might like to check, using a small set of scores, that $\Sigma (X - \bar{X})^2$ works out to the same answer as $\Sigma X^2 - (\Sigma X)^2/N$

Take especial care not to confuse ΣX^2 – where you first of all square the scores and then afterwards add these squares together; and $(\Sigma X)^2$ – where you first add together all the scores and then square the total.

Step-by-step procedure

Standard deviation

What to calculate	How to calculate it	Usual symbols
Step 1 total	Add all the observations together	ΣX
Step 2 mean	Divide the result of **step 1** by the number of observations	$\dfrac{\Sigma X}{N} = \bar{X}$
Step 3 uncorrected sum of squares	(a) Square each of the observations	X^2
	(b) Add all the squares together	ΣX^2
Step 4 correction term	(a) Go back to the total obtained in **step 1** and square it	$(\Sigma X)^2$
	(b) Divide the result of **step 4a** by the number of observations	$\dfrac{(\Sigma X)^2}{N}$
Step 5 corrected sum of squares	Subtract the result of **step 4b** from that of **step 3b**	$\Sigma X^2 - \dfrac{(\Sigma X)^2}{N}$
Step 6 variance	Divide the result of **step 5** by (number of observations − 1) NB $(N-1)$ is often referred to as 'degrees of freedom'	$\dfrac{\Sigma X^2 - (\Sigma X)^2/N}{(N-1)}$
Step 7 standard deviation	Take the square root of the result of **step 6**	$\sqrt{\dfrac{\Sigma X^2 - (\Sigma X)^2/N}{(N-1)}}$

Worked example

Standard deviation

	Observations		Step 3a $(Observations)^2$
	4·5		20·25
	6·0		36·00
	7·4		54·76
	8·2		67·24
	2·1		4·41
	6·5		42·25
	5·4		29·16
	9·3		86·49
	10·8		116·64
	8·0	Step 3b	64·00
	———	uncorrected	———
Step 1 total =	68·2	sum of squares =	521·20

Step 2 mean $= \dfrac{68·2}{10} = 6·82$

Step 4a $= (68·2)^2$

Step 4b
correction term $= \dfrac{(68·2)^2}{10} = \dfrac{4651·2}{10} = 465·12$

Step 5 corrected
sum of squares $= 521·20 - 465·12 = 56·08$

Step 6 variance $= \dfrac{56·08}{9} = 6·23$

Step 7 standard
variation $= \sqrt{6·23} = 2·5$

Standard scores

For the purpose of comparison, say, of different individuals on some test or of the same individual on different tests, it is often useful to transform scores into **standard scores** (or **z-scores**) by expressing the scores in terms of standard deviation units:

$$\text{standard score } z = \frac{\text{deviation score } x}{\text{standard deviation}}$$

where the deviation score is the difference between the individual score and the mean,

i.e. $x = X - \overline{X}$.

When all scores in a set are transformed into z-scores, the distribution is said to be standardized. This point will be returned to in the next chapter in connection with the normal distribution.

Correlation

We have been considering so far in this chapter the ways in which data on a single variable may be summarized by using measures of central tendency and of dispersion. There are very many occasions when we are interested in not just one variable by itself but rather on how it is related to, or connected with, a second variable.

In talking about an experiment we necessarily talk about two variables of course – the independent variable and the dependent variable. Obviously one might wish to describe not only the distribution of scores on the dependent variable, as we have been doing above, but also to describe the relationship between the two variables.

One can describe both the degree (or closeness) and the direction of such a relationship by what is called a **correlation coefficient**. The size of the correlation coefficient tells us something about the degree of relationship. It has values from zero, indicating a complete lack of relationship, to one, for a perfect relationship. A plus or minus before the numerical value of the correlation coefficient indicates the direction of the relationship. Thus, a positive correlation indicates that the larger scores on one variable tend to be paired with the larger scores on the other variable; a negative correlation indicates that the larger scores on one variable tend to be paired with the smaller scores on the other variable.

The scattergram

The idea behind correlation can be seen more clearly if we plot out the data in graphical form. One variable is represented by the horizontal (X) dimension, the other by the vertical (Y) dimension. When these variables are the independent variable and the dependent variable, the convention used *on any graph* is to plot the independent variable on the horizontal axis and the dependent variable on the vertical axis.

However, in considering correlation, it is not essential that we have a clear-cut distinction between independent and dependent variables. In fact, there is no necessity for the measures to be obtained from an actual experiment. The most common situation that you are likely to come across is where a set of subjects is observed, and each subject is given a measure on the two variables.

Thus, suppose that for a class of children we obtain measures of their heights and weights. A correlation coefficient will tell us how closely these two variables are related. It is very important to note that, even when a strong relationship is found, it does not necessarily mean that changes in one variable cause changes in the second variable.

In plotting a scattergram, the scores of a particular subject are marked on the graph by a dot, X units to the right along the horizontal axis and Y units up the vertical axis. Thus a subject with height 135 cm and weight 31 kg would be represented as shown in Figure 7.

For a set of subjects, the scattergram might look like Figure 8. A glance at this scattergram suggests that there is some relationship between the variables – tall children do tend to be heavier. This is an example of a positive correlation in that high scores on one of the variables tend to be associated with high scores on the second variable. Examples of different kinds of relationship are shown in Figure 9.

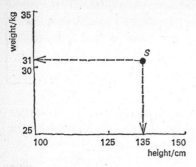

Figure 7 Representation on a scattergram of a subject with height 135 cm and weight 31 kg

An alternative way of looking at correlation is to say that a high degree of correlation enables us to make accurate predictions about the scores on one variable when the scores on the other variable are known. Notice that this applies with equal force for positive and negative correlations. If there is a strong negative correlation, it simply means that we predict low scores on one variable from a knowledge of high scores on the other variable.

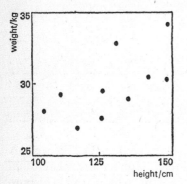

Figure 8 An example of a scattergram

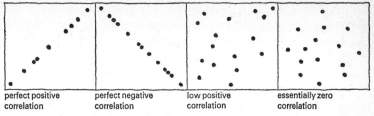

| perfect positive correlation | perfect negative correlation | low positive correlation | essentially zero correlation |

Figure 9 Scattergrams for different degrees of correlation

Spearman's rho

Several correlation coefficients have been developed. We will cover just one of these here, Spearman's rho (ϱ), otherwise known as Spearman's rank order correlation coefficient. Appendix 2 gives details of a second correlation coefficient, Pearson's r.

Spearman's rho is based on rank orders. It deals, not with the scores themselves, but with the order of these scores when they have been ranked in size. There are, of course, some situations where ranks or orderings are all that we have. Say that we can measure preferences within a set of things so that one of them is placed first (given rank one), another is placed second (given rank two) and so on. Spearman's rho can also be used in situations like this where the data are in the form of ranks from the start.

Suppose we have two people ranking a set of eight politicians on some quality, say honesty. The ranks may be as follows:

Table 7 Rankings of politicians' honesty given by two persons

	Rank given to politician							
	A	*B*	*C*	*D*	*E*	*F*	*G*	*H*
person 1	1	2	3	4	5	6	7	8
person 2	1	4	2	5	8	6	3	7

We have taken the first person's ordering as the basis and shown how the second person compares – thus they agree about who is most honest, but the politician ranked second by the first person is ranked fourth by the second person. In attempting to measure the degree of correlation between these rankings it is clear that if they are perfectly correlated we either have the rankings given by the two persons identical (a perfect positive correlation), or that one ranking is the reverse of the other where what person one ranks first is ranked eighth by person two and so on (a perfect negative correlation).

Spearman's rho is based upon the amount of disagreement between the two rankings. Specifically, the measure used is the sum of the squared difference in ranks (i.e. Σd^2, where d is the difference in rankings for each of the things ranked).

In the example given above, $d = 0$ for politician A, $d = -2$ for politician B, $d = 1$ for politician C, etc. and

$$\Sigma\ d^2 = 0^2 + (-2)^2 + 1^2 + (-1)^2 + (-3)^2 + 0^2 + 4^2 + 1^2 = 32.$$

It is clear that Σd^2 will be a minimum, in fact zero, when the two rankings are identical. Similarly it is clear that Σd^2 will be a maximum when one rank order is the exact reverse of the other. Hence the equation

$$\text{Spearman's rho } (\varrho) = 1 - \frac{2\ \Sigma\ d^2}{\left(\begin{array}{c}\text{maximum value}\\ \text{of } \Sigma\ d^2\end{array}\right)}$$

gives a correlation coefficient of $+1$ when there is no disagreement ($\Sigma d^2 = 0$) and a correlation coefficient of -1 where the disagreement is a maximum. You can check this by substituting

$$\Sigma d^2 = (\text{maximum value of } \Sigma\ d^2)$$

into the equation for Spearman's rho.

It is not unreasonable to think of a total lack of correlation as being half-way between these two extremes of perfect agreement and perfect disagreement. If we take the value of Σd^2 as half of its maximum value, you find that this produces a value of zero for Spearman's rho. If Σd^2 is less than half its maximum a positive correlation results; if more than half there will be a negative correlation.

While the equation given above is not difficult to use, a version which looks rather different is more commonly used. This relies on the fact that the maximum value of Σd^2 can be worked out directly from N, the number of things ranked.

$$\text{Spearman's rho } (\varrho) = 1 - \frac{6 \, \Sigma \, d^2}{N(N^2 - 1)}$$

where $\Sigma \; d^2$ is the sum of the squared differences in rank and $N =$ the number of pairs of ranks.

It must be stressed that Spearman's rho is a descriptive statistic; it simply describes the direction and degree of the relationship between the variables. It is, however, possible to assess the significance of the relationship between the variables in a similar way to that discussed with the sign test (p. 45). Table C gives figures for the smallest values of Spearman's rho significant at the 0·05 level of significance for different numbers of pairs of scores.

If ϱ exceeds the table value for the number of pairs of scores in the experiment, then there is a significant agreement between the rankings under the two conditions (at the $p = 0.05$ level). If ϱ does not exceed the table value, then there is no significant agreement between the rankings under the two conditions (at the $p = 0.05$ level).

Step-by-step procedure

Spearman's rho

Step 1 Rank data (for each group separately) giving rank 1 to the highest score, and so on
Note If two or more scores in a group are the same then give the average rank for these tied scores

Step 2 Obtain the difference (d) between each pair of ranks $\qquad d$

Step 3 Square each of the differences $\qquad d^2$

Step 4 Add all the squares together $\qquad \Sigma d^2$

Step 5 Calculate $N \times (N^2 - 1)$ where N is the number of pairs of scores $\qquad N(N^2 - 1)$

Step 6
$$\varrho = 1 - \frac{6 \Sigma d^2}{N(N^2 - 1)}$$

Step 7 If required, assess the significance of ϱ using Table C

Step 8 Translate the result back in terms of the experiment.

Note The procedure can be followed if the data is given directly in the form of ranks by simply omitting Step 1

Worked example

Spearman's rho

Subject	Scores	
	A	B
subject 1	3	5
subject 2	7	9
subject 3	3	7
subject 4	12	11
subject 5	8	11
subject 6	14	11

Step 1	ranks		Step 2	Step 3
Subject	A	B	d	d^2
subject 1	5·5	6	−0·5	0·25
subject 2	4	4	0	0
subject 3	5·5	5	0·5	0·25
subject 4	2	2	0	0
subject 5	3	2	1	1
subject 6	1	2	−1	1

Step 4 $\Sigma\ d^2 = 2.50$

Step 5 $N \times (N^2 - 1) = 6 \times (36 - 1) = 210$.

Step 6

$$\varrho = 1 - \frac{6\Sigma d^2}{N(N^2 - 1)} = 1 - \frac{6 \times 2.50}{210}$$

$$= 1 - 0.07 = + 0.93$$

Step 7 From Table C, ϱ must exceed 0·83 for $N = 6$. As $\varrho = 0.93$ there is a significant agreement between the two orderings of the data at the $p = 0.05$ level

Step 8 There is a significant positive correlation ($\varrho = + 0.93$) between the scores on the two variables

Note Spearman's rho should be treated with caution when there is a high proportion of ties as in this example

5 The normal distribution and distributions associated with it

We have made use of the histogram on several occasions so far to give us a pictorial or graphical view of how a set of scores is distributed. Let us take as an example the distribution of heights of children of a given age. This distribution might look something like Figure 10. Each bar of the histogram represents a height range of fifteen centimetres. There is no compelling reason why this range should be chosen. It could be smaller; indeed, the interval could be as small as one liked. A variable of this type, which can be continuously sub-divided, is called a **continuous** variable. There are other variables, which can only take on particular values, called

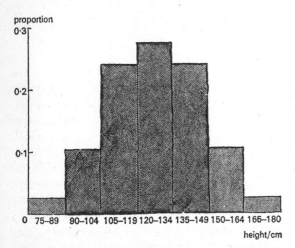

Figure 10 Histogram showing proportion of children with different heights

discrete variables (e.g. size of family). By reducing the size of the interval, the rectangles increase in number and become thinner so that the histogram approximates to a smooth curve when there is a sufficiently large sample (Figure 11). It then becomes possible in many cases to express the distribution very neatly and succinctly by simply giving the mathematical formula for the curve.

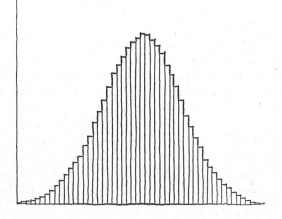

Figure 11   Approximation of a histogram to a smooth curve as the interval decreases

One such curve which you will hear referred to frequently is the **normal distribution curve**. As its properties were first investigated by Gauss, it is also commonly known as the **Gaussian** distribution. Incidentally, there is nothing abnormal or peculiar about other distribution curves – it just so happens that the so-called 'normal' curve is one which crops up so many times and which has particularly useful, simple, and well-known mathematical properties. Different normal distributions vary only in their means and standard deviations and hence, if they are standardized so that they have the same mean and standard deviation, they have identical shapes. This intimate relationship between the standard deviation and the normal distribution is one of the reasons for the widespread use of the standard deviation.

The importance of the normal distribution

1 On theoretical grounds

It can be shown theoretically that, if we assume that there are very many small errors all operating independently of each other, then the resulting distribution is the normal distribution and, as we have discussed previously, it appears likely that in psychology many of the measurements that we wish to make will be subject to just this kind of random error.

2 On practical grounds

In fact if a sufficiently large number of observations or measurements are made so that the shape of the distribution can be assessed, it will very frequently transpire that the distribution does actually approximate more or less closely to the normal distribution. For example, human height is distributed in this way and, so some have argued, is human intelligence.

3 On mathematical grounds

It has been pointed out that the normal distribution is particularly simple mathematically. In fact there are many problems in mathematical statistics which are only soluble in terms of a normal distribution. What is important practically is that the results obtained by using a normal distribution often apply quite well, even when the distribution differs somewhat from the normal.

There is a very useful and general theorem, based on probability theory, called the **central limit theorem**. This states that the distribution of means of samples taken from any population will tend towards the normal distribution as the size of the samples taken increases.

The shape of the normal distribution curve

The shape of the normal distribution curve is illustrated in Figure 12. It is bell-shaped and is symmetrical about its mean; that is, if one imagines a vertical line down through the mean, then the shapes on either side of the line are identical. The median and mode occur at the same value as the mean. The curve falls away relatively slowly at first on either side of the mean. In other words, there is a high probability of scores occurring just a little above or just a little below the mean. When one gets to the 'tail' of the distribution, either above or below the mean, the curve approaches the horizontal axis asymptotically; that is, the slope of the curve decreases continually for values further and further from the mean so that, although the axis is approached, it is never actually reached (although this is impossible to show on a drawing such as Figure 12). What this means is that there will be a finite non-zero probability of occurrence even for values a long way from the mean.

The standard deviation is associated with the curve in the following way. If we consider an upper limit obtained by going one standard deviation above the mean, and a lower limit obtained by going one standard deviation below the mean, a certain proportion of the population will be contained within these limits. For the normal distribution, this proportion is 0·6826, that is, 68·26 per cent of the scores in any normal distribution fall within the limits of one standard deviation above and below the mean. If we consider wider limits, say two standard deviations above and below the mean, then the shape of the normal distribution is such that 95·44 per cent of the scores fall within these limits; for plus and minus three standard deviations, this percentage rises to 99·73 per cent.

To take an example, if it is known that the mean of a population is

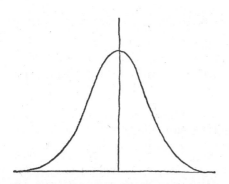

Figure 12 The normal distribution curve

100 (say the population is one of IQs which are standardized to a mean of 100) and the standard deviation is 15, then we know that 68·26 per cent of the population will lie within limits of 115 to 85, 95·44 per cent within limits of 130 to 70 and 99·73 per cent within limits of 145 to 55.

Standard normal distribution

As was pointed out in the last chapter, standard scores (z-scores) can be obtained by expressing scores in terms of standard deviation units,

i.e. standard score $z = \dfrac{\text{deviation score } x}{\text{standard deviation}}$.

Tables of the normal distribution are usually given in this standard form. Table D is an example which shows the fractional area under the standard normal curve. It can be seen from this table that for a z-score of 1·0, the fractional area enclosed between the mean of the distribution (where $z = 0$) and $z = 1·0$ is 0·3413. As the curve is symmetrical, the area which would be enclosed between z-scores of $-1·0$ and $+1·0$ is therefore $2 \times 0·3413 = 0·6826$. Another way of expressing this is to say that a proportion of 0·6826 (i.e. approximately 68 per cent) is contained within these limits – which is what was stated in the last section.

Taking a different example of the use of Table D, look at the area corresponding to a z-score of 1·96. The table shows that this is 0·4750. Therefore between the limits of $z = -1·96$ and $z = +1·96$, a fractional area of $2 \times 0·4750 = 0·95$ (95 per cent) is contained. This means, of course, that 5 per cent of the population exceeds these limits.

Hence, in an experimental situation where we can establish that we are dealing with the normal distribution, a z-score exceeding 1·96 can be used to demonstrate that the IV had an effect on the DV at the 5 per cent level of significance. Use the table to find the z-score corresponding to the 1 per cent level of significance.

Samples and populations

In an experiment, what we are doing is taking a set of scores and we will almost invariably be regarding these scores as a sample taken from some population.

By appropriate randomization techniques, we try to make sure that each member of the population has an equal chance of appearing in the sample. This then means that the results obtained from the sample can be generalized to the population.

You may be worried about the way in which we have been using the words 'sample' and 'population'. In statistics they are not limited to references to people. Thus one talks about samples and populations of scores, as well as samples and populations of people.

When standard deviation was being discussed earlier, it was pointed out that the formula we used was appropriate for obtaining estimates of the *population* standard deviation from the scores in the sample. Thus, if from our sample we obtain a value of 80 for the mean and 10 for the standard deviation, then our estimate is that in the population from which the sample is drawn, 68 per cent of the scores will lie between the limits of 70 to 90.

This is only an estimate, of course. We have no certainty that it is correct. But it does mean that, if at a later stage we obtain a score of 56, it would be quite improbable that it came from the same population (after all we estimate that approximately 95 per cent of the scores lie between 60 and 100, i.e. between plus and minus two standard deviations). It would not be impossible, however, for it to come from the population – remember those tails approaching the horizontal axis asymptotically.

A problem which we are much more likely to be concerned with in attempting to evaluate the results of our experiments is the decision as to whether the scores obtained under one experimental treatment or condition differ from the scores obtained under another experimental treatment or condition. We have already considered one way in which a decision could be reached – by using the sign test – but there ought to be a way which would make direct use of the actual scores which we obtain. What we would really like to know is whether the difference in the *mean* scores of the two experimental *samples* can be taken as evidence that there is a genuine difference between the two experimental conditions. The question is a familiar one. Is the observed difference in means sufficiently unlikely when random errors alone are acting that we are willing to decide that something else apart from the random errors is having an effect; in other words that the IV is affecting the DV?

In order to attack this problem, we have to consider a special kind of standard deviation called the **standard error**.

Standard error

Suppose that we take as a population the actual population of adults in the world. And further suppose that we take a random sample of 1000 people and measure their heights. (The actual procedure necessary to get a random sample is left to the fertile imagination of the reader, as I am not sure that I could do it. Remember that each individual must have an equal chance of ending up in the sample.) The distribution might look something like Figure 13. Flushed by our success, we gather in a second sample of 1000 and measure again. This time we might find that the mean of the distribution was slightly higher, say 167 cm. Repeating the process again with a third sample would lead to a slightly different mean again and so on. The point I am trying to make is that we would not obtain identical means from successive samples. There would be a certain amount of variation, in fact if one were to sample repeatedly in this way, taking

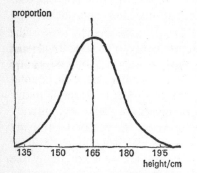

Figure 13 Distribution of heights for a sample of 1000 people (fictitious data)

1000 people at a time, it would be possible to build up a **sampling distribution** of the **mean** scores. We could draw up a curve showing the frequency of occurrence of different mean scores, and it might look something like Figure 14. If this is compared with the sampling distribution of the scores themselves, it can be seen that there is much less variability in the mean scores than in the single scores. An alternative way of putting this is to say that the standard deviation of the means is considerably less than the standard deviation of the scores themselves. *The standard deviation of the means is given a special name. It is called the* **standard error**.

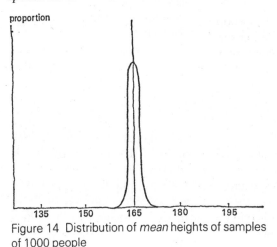

proportion

135   150   165   180   195

Figure 14 Distribution of *mean* heights of samples of 1000 people

It is common sense that the means will vary less than the individual scores – in fact mathematically there is a very simple and neat relationship between the standard error (SE) and the standard deviation (SD) of the scores:

$$SE = \frac{SD}{\sqrt{N}},$$

where *N* is the size of sample (1000 in the example quoted above).

The *t*-test

Let us say that, in an experiment, the mean score for condition A exceeded that for condition B where A and B are two levels of a particular independent variable. Are we justified then in saying that the IV is affecting the DV? This is, once again, the question of generalizing from the sample of experimental results to the population. Two factors which would influence our decision are, firstly, the size of the difference in means and, secondly, the amount of variability in the scores. The bigger the difference in means, the more confidence we have that the sample difference reflects a real difference between the experimental conditions, but the larger the variability in scores, the less is our confidence.

These two factors are taken into account in the so-called *t*-test, where

$$t = \frac{\text{difference in means}}{\text{standard error of the difference in means}}.$$

Previously, we have talked about the standard error as being the name given to the standard deviation of the mean; this can be generalized to indicate the standard error of the difference in two means. If we draw two samples from a single population and look at the means of the two samples, we will find that almost always there will be some difference in the mean scores. Sometimes the difference will be negligible.

By taking repeated pairs of samples and each time noting the difference in the means of the two samples, it will be possible to plot the sampling distribution of the difference in means in a similar manner to that in which the sampling distribution of the means was built up in Figure 14. An example of what this might look like is shown in Figure 15.

By the way, do not be worried that you are going to have to spend the rest of your life painstakingly building up sampling distributions by taking sample after sample. By using statistical theory it is possible, after making certain assumptions about the population and sample, to derive formulae for the sampling distributions.

Do not be upset that Figure 15 looks very different from Figure 14. By choosing an appropriate scale for Figure 15, both figures

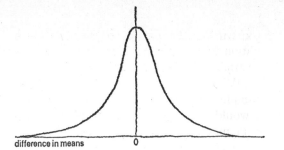

difference in means   0

Figure 15 Sampling distribution of difference in means of two samples taken from the same population

could be made to look very much the same. The point made by drawing Figures 13 and 14 to the same horizontal scale is that the sampling distribution of individual scores is much wider than the sampling distribution of mean scores. Similarly, the sampling distribution for difference in individual scores would be much wider than the sampling distribution for difference in means if it were drawn to the same horizontal scale as Figure 15.

It is perhaps strange that, if the samples drawn from the population are relatively small (say 50 or less), then the sampling distribution of *t* is not normal, although the underlying population is itself normal. The distribution is in fact known as the *t*-distribution and differs slightly in shape from the normal distribution. In accordance with the central limit theorem mentioned earlier (p. 70), the *t*-distribution tends towards the normal distribution as sample size increases.

Let us say that the observed difference in means in a particular experiment is as shown in Figure 16. If the samples are drawn from identical populations, this difference in means is unlikely to occur; as you can see, it takes us into one of the tails of the distribution.

But, is it sufficiently improbable for us to come to the decision that the independent variable did have an effect on the dependent variable?

The way in which we come to this decision is identical to the way in which we came to a decision for the sign test. We decide on a significance level. Remember that the significance level is the

77

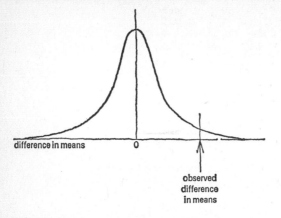

difference in means   0

observed
difference
in means

Figure 16   Observed difference in means superimposed
on the sampling distribution of Figure 15

probability of making a type 1 error, i.e. the probability of deciding
that the independent variable had an effect on the dependent
variable when this is not the case. If we chose the conventional
significance level of 5 per cent, what this amounts to is cutting off 5
per cent of the t-distribution. This has been done in Figure 17. Here
the distribution is divided into a **central region**, where the decision is
made that the IV had no effect on the DV; and the **two tails** (shaded
in the figure) where the decision is made that the IV did have an
effect on the DV. What value of difference in means do we take as
the critical value, i.e. the one which is exceeded by 5 per cent of the
population? This is already tabulated for us as the t-distribution
(Table E).

    As discussed above, the t statistic is the difference in means
divided by the standard error. An alternative way of regarding this
is as a difference in means measured in units of standard error. A t of
2 indicates that the difference in means is twice the standard error,
and so on. A feature of the t-distribution is that it changes shape
somewhat as the size of the sample changes. This means that the
critical 5 per cent value changes with the sample size (which is
related to the d.f. – degrees of freedom – of Table E).

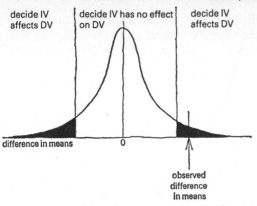

decide IV
affects DV

decide IV has no effect
on DV

decide IV
affects DV

difference in means   0

observed
difference
in means

Figure 17   Cut-off points added to Figure 16

Computation of *t*

The computation of *t* differs according to whether we are using an independent-subjects design on the one hand, or a matched-subjects or repeated-measures design on the other hand (see pp. 28–30).

Assumptions underlying the *t*-test

In deriving the *t*-distribution, certain assumptions have to be made about the populations from which the samples are drawn. These are that the population distributions are **normal** and of the **same variance** (sometimes called the **homogeneity of variance** assumption). It is possible to test for the reasonableness of these assumptions. The **chi-square** test (Chapter 6) can be used as a test of 'goodness of fit' to a normal distribution. (The details of how this is done are not given in Chapter 6. They are available in more advanced texts, e.g. Hays (1973).) The **variance-ratio** test (discussed later) can be used to test the homogeneity of variance assumption.

However, statisticians have demonstrated that the *t*-test is extremely **robust** with respect to violation of these assumptions. This means there can be considerable deviation from normality and/or homogeneity of variance without the result of the *t*-test being affected. An exception to this is with the independent-samples design when there are different numbers of scores under the two experimental conditions. Here, violations of the homogeneity of variance assumptions can be serious, and it is worthwhile to test this assumption (using the variance-ratio test) before carrying out the t-test.

The strategy recommended for all other cases is to examine the data and then, unless there are glaring deviations from either normality or from homogeneity of variance, go ahead with the t-test.

One-tail and two-tail tests

We divided the distribution into a region where the decision was made that the IV *was* affecting the DV and a region where the decision was made that the IV *was not* affecting the DV. Both tails of the distribution were considered as regions where we would decide that the IV was having an effect. Hence we are willing to conclude that there is an effect if we have a sufficiently large difference in means (with respect to its standard error) either in one direction or the other. This is commonly referred to as a **two-tailed test** (i.e. we are simply testing for a difference in population means under the two experimental conditions). In terms of Hypotheses we are testing the Null Hypothesis that there is no difference in means, against a general or non-directional Alternative Hypothesis that there *is* a difference in means.

There may be some situations where we have a good reason for specifying the expected direction of the difference between the means. This reason may be theoretical, that is, it comes out as a prediction from a theory, or it may be from previous work done in the area or, in some cases, just common sense. For instance, if we compare the problem-solving abilities of normal monkeys with those of monkeys with brain lesions (i.e. ones with part of the brain removed) then we might well start out with a hypothesis that the normal monkeys will perform better than the lesioned animals. In these cases, use can be made of a **one-tail** test. The reason for the name is obvious – we are dealing with only one of the tails of the distribution. In this case the Null Hypothesis that there is no difference in means is being tested against a directional Alternative Hypothesis that condition A (say) has a higher mean than condition B.

We will, if we are using a one-tail test, only decide that the IV has affected the DV if the experimental result falls at one end of the distribution. This means that the critical 5 per cent *t*-value for a two-tail test becomes a 2·5 per cent critical value if a one-tail test is used. This is because the 5 per cent value in the table means that 5 per cent of the distribution occurs in the two tails taken together, and hence that there is 2·5 per cent in each of the separate tails. Hence, if we wish to use the conventional 5 per cent significance level in conjunction with a one-tail test, we must use the 10 per cent value in the table. These values are not shown in Table E but are available in books of Statistical Tables.

Because of this, it can happen that a result which would not be significant if a two-tail test is used becomes significant if a one-tail test is used. Whilst this seems somewhat fishy, remember that the decision about what kind of hypothesis you are dealing with should be made *before* doing the experiment and not after. There are people who argue that two-tail tests should always be used and, starting out on experimentation as you are, it is wise to deal almost exclusively in terms of two-tail tests. Remember that if you have a one-tail test and the result comes out in the opposite direction to that hypothesized, then one cannot conclude that the IV had an effect on the DV, even in cases where the difference in means is large.

Significance Revisited

By this time you should be getting more of a feel of the meaning of statistical significance. If you are not you should skip back to p. 41 and review this. It is perhaps appropriate to add a word of warning here. In common usage 'significant' means 'important'. However statistical significance simply tells us that something is unlikely to have happened by chance. This in itself tells us little about the practical importance of the effect which we have found. In particular you should note that by increasing the sample size, that is by collecting more data, you are going to make it more likely to get a statistically significant result. This appears intuitively clear in the case of the t-test where increasing the sample size (N) has the effect of decreasing the standard error ($= SD/\sqrt{N}$) and hence of increasing the value of t ($=$ difference in means/SE).

Another way of putting this is to appreciate that with a sufficiently large sample size one can get a significant value of t with a very small difference in means. In practical terms this difference in means may be trivial, particularly if we have a complex situation where other variables are more important. So, the general message is that statistical significance is not all-important and, once again, that you cannot afford to switch off your common-sense when interpreting the results of experiments.

Step-by-step procedure

t-Test – independent samples

Use with independent-subject design
(NB **steps A1–5** and **B1–5** are identical to **steps 1–5** of the standard deviation procedure, p. 58.)

Step A1	Add all A observations together	ΣX_A
Step A2	Divide **A1** (i.e. the result of **step A1**) by the number of A observations N_A	$\dfrac{\Sigma X_A}{N_A} = \overline{X}_A$
Step A3	(a) Square each of the A observations	X_A^2
	(b) Add all the squares together	ΣX_A^2
Step A4	(a) Square **A1**	$(\Sigma X_A)^2$
	(b) Divide **A4a** by N_A	$\dfrac{(\Sigma X_A)^2}{N_A}$
Step A5	Subtract **A4b** from **A3b**	$\Sigma X_A^2 - \dfrac{(\Sigma X_A)^2}{N_A}$

Steps B1–5 Repeat the above 5 steps for the B observations

Worked example

t-Test – independent samples

	A observation	Step A3a $(A\ observation)^2$	B observation
	3	9	6
	5	25	5
	2	4	7
	4	16	8
	6	36	9
	2	4	4
	7	49	7
	—	—	8
Step A1 $\Sigma X_A = 29$		**Step A3b** $\Sigma X_A^2 = 143$	9
			7

Step A2 $\overline{X}_A = \dfrac{29}{7} = 4.14$

Step A4a $(\Sigma X_A)^2 = 29^2$

Step A4b $\dfrac{(\Sigma X_A)^2}{N_A} = \dfrac{29^2}{7} = 120.1$

Step A5 $\Sigma X_A^2 - \dfrac{(\Sigma X_A)^2}{N_A} = 143 - 120.1 = 22.9$

Step B1 $\Sigma X_B = (6 + 5 + 7 + 8 + 9 + 4 + 7 + 8 + 9 + 7)$
$\qquad = 70$

Step B2 $\overline{X}_B = \dfrac{70}{10} = 7$

Step B3 $\Sigma X_B^2 = (36 + 25 + 49 + 64 + 81 + 16 + 49 + 64 + 81 + 49) = 514$

Step B4a $(\Sigma X_B)^2 = 70^2$

Step B4b $\dfrac{(\Sigma X_B)^2}{N_B} = \dfrac{70^2}{10} = 490$

Step B5 $\Sigma X_B^2 - \dfrac{(\Sigma X_B)^2}{N_B} = 514 - 490 = 24$

t-Test – independent samples

Step 6 Add **A5** and **B5**

$$\left[\Sigma X_A^2 - \frac{(\Sigma X_A)^2}{N_A}\right] + \left[\Sigma X_B^2 - \frac{(\Sigma X_B)^2}{N_B}\right]$$

Step 7 Divide **6** by N_A minus 1 added to N_B minus 1

$$\frac{[\Sigma X_A^2 - (\Sigma X_A)^2/N_A] + [\Sigma X_B^2 - (\Sigma X_B)^2/N_B]}{(N_A - 1) + (N_B - 1)}$$

Step 8 Find the reciprocal of N_A and the reciprocal of N_B and add them together

$$\frac{1}{N_A} + \frac{1}{N_B}$$

Step 9 Multiply **7** by **8**

$$\frac{[\Sigma X_A^2 - (\Sigma X_A)^2/N_A] + [\Sigma X_B^2 - (\Sigma X_B)^2/N_B]}{(N_A - 1) + (N_B - 1)} \times$$

$$\left(\frac{1}{N_A} + \frac{1}{N_B}\right)$$

Step 10 Take the square root of **9**

Step 11 Take the difference between **A2** and **B2**

$$\bar{X}_A - \bar{X}_B$$

Step 12 Divide **11** by **10**: the result is *t*!!

$$t = (\bar{X}_A - \bar{X}_B)$$

$$\div \sqrt{\left[\frac{\{\Sigma X_A^2 - (\Sigma X_A)^2/N_A\} + \{\Sigma X_B^2 - (\Sigma X_B)^2/N_B\}}{(N_A - 1) + (N_B - 1)} \times \left(\frac{1}{N_A} + \frac{1}{N_B}\right)\right]}$$

with $(N_A - 1) + (N_B - 1)$ degrees of freedom

Step 13 Translate the result back in terms of the experiment

Worked example – continued

t-Test – independent samples

Step 6 $22 \cdot 9 + 24 = 46 \cdot 9$

Step 7 $\dfrac{46 \cdot 9}{(7-1)+(10-1)} = \dfrac{46 \cdot 9}{15} = 3 \cdot 13$

Step 8 $(\frac{1}{7} + \frac{1}{10}) = (0 \cdot 1429 + 0 \cdot 1000) = 0 \cdot 2429$

Step 9 $3 \cdot 13 \times 0 \cdot 2429 = 0 \cdot 760$

Step 10 $\sqrt{0 \cdot 760} = 0 \cdot 872$

Step 11 $4 \cdot 14 - 7 = -2 \cdot 86$

Step 12 $t = -\dfrac{2 \cdot 86}{0 \cdot 872} = -3 \cdot 28$

with $(7-1)+(10-1) = 15$ degrees of freedom
From Table E, $t = 2 \cdot 13$ at the $0 \cdot 05$ level of significance
(i.e. $p = 5$ per cent) with 15 degrees of freedom

Step 13 We therefore conclude that the IV had an effect on the DV, as the observed value of t is numerically greater than $2 \cdot 13$

Step-by-step procedure

t-Test – correlated samples

Use with matched-subject or repeated-measures design

Step 1	Obtain the difference (d) between each pair of scores	$d = (X_A - X_B)$
Step 2	Add all the differences together	Σd
Step 3	Divide 2 (i.e. the result of **step 2**) by the number of pairs of scores (n)	$\dfrac{\Sigma d}{n} = \bar{d}$
Step 4	(a) Square each of the differences (b) Add all the squares together	d^2 Σd^2
Step 5	(a) Square 2 (b) Divide **5a** by n	$(\Sigma d)^2$ $\dfrac{(\Sigma d)^2}{n}$
Step 6	Subtract **5b** from **4b**	$\Sigma d^2 - \dfrac{(\Sigma d)^2}{n}$
Step 7	Divide **6** by $n(n-1)$	$\dfrac{\Sigma d^2 - (\Sigma d)^2/n}{n(n-1)}$
Step 8	Take the square root of **7**	
Step 9	Divide **3** by **8**: the result is t $t = \bar{d} \div \sqrt{\dfrac{\Sigma d^2 - (\Sigma d)^2/n}{n(n-1)}}$ with $(n-1)$ degrees of freedom	
Step 10	Translate the result of the test back in terms of the experiment	

Worked example

t-Test – correlated samples

The data represents scores obtained by 7 people in a certain test with and without the presence of a drug

Subject	Scores with	Scores without	Step 1 d	Step 4a d^2
1	3	6	3	9
2	8	14	6	36
3	4	8	4	16
4	6	4	−2	4
5	9	16	7	49
6	2	7	5	25
7	12	19	7	49

Step 2 $\Sigma\, d = 30$

Step 3 $\dfrac{\Sigma\, d}{n} = \overline{d} = \dfrac{30}{7} = 4\cdot29$

Step 4b $\Sigma\, d^2 = 188$

Step 5a $(\Sigma\, d)^2 = 30^2 = 900$

Step 5b $\dfrac{(\Sigma\, d)^2}{n} = \dfrac{900}{7} = 128\cdot57$

Step 6 $\Sigma\, d^2 - \dfrac{(\Sigma\, d)^2}{n} = 188 - 128\cdot57 = 59\cdot43$

Step 7 $\dfrac{\Sigma\, d^2 - (\Sigma\, d)^2/n}{n(n-1)} = \dfrac{59\cdot43}{7 \times 6} = 1\cdot41$

Step 8 $\sqrt{1\cdot41} = 1\cdot19$

Step 9 $t = \overline{d} \div \sqrt{\dfrac{\Sigma\, d^2 - (\Sigma\, d)^2/n}{n(n-1)}} = \dfrac{4\cdot29}{1\cdot19} = 3\cdot61$

with $(7-1) = 6$ degrees of freedom
From Table E, $\underline{t = 2\cdot45}$ at the $0\cdot05$ level of significance, with 6 degrees of freedom

Step 10 We therefore conclude that the IV had an effect on the DV, as the observed t is numerically greater than $2\cdot45$: the drug produced a significant decrease in mean score on this test ($t = 3\cdot61$ with 6 d.f. Significant at the 5 per cent level)

The variance-ratio test (F-test)

In the discussion above, we have been concerned with hypotheses about differences in means between two conditions. Although many behavioural hypotheses can be translated into statistical hypotheses about means, there are others where the appropriate statistical hypothesis is concerned with the relative dispersion of scores under two conditions. The variance-ratio test (or F-test) is suitable for these situations.

(What is variance? If you have forgotten or are not sure return to p. 55.)

As an example, consider performance in some task with the preferred hand as against the non-preferred hand. Suppose we get our subjects to play shove ha'penny with the preferred hand on some occasions, the non-preferred hand on others. One obvious way of comparing performance with the two hands would be by comparing the variability in aiming by the two hands – i.e. by using the variance-ratio test to compare the two variances.

There are several possibilities as to how you might get the actual scores, but I will leave this to your ingenuity. Comparing variability or spread by a variance-ratio test is not the only thing that you could do, of course. An alternative would be to look at the mean error, i.e. how much the target is overshot or undershot. You would then have to consider whether to take undershoots separately from overshoots. Are you going to call one lot positive and the other negative, or are you going to ignore the sign and call an overshoot of 1 cm the same as an undershoot of 1 cm? What you decide will be determined by exactly what hypothesis you have. One can note, however, that ignoring the signs and looking at the mean scores gives an alternative method of assessing the variability of scores to that of looking at variance.

You should note that the values shown in Table F relate to significance for a two-tailed test. Many books of tables give values for a one-tailed test which are appropriate for other uses of the variance-ratio test.

Assumptions underlying the variance-ratio test

As with the t-test, the variance-ratio test makes assumptions about the underlying population distribution. Again the assumption is of normality. However, once again, the test is robust and the recommended action is to carry on with the variance-ratio test unless the distributions are very far from normal.

Step-by-step procedure

Variance-ratio test (_F_-test)

Step 1 Obtain the variance separately for each set of scores (use the standard deviation step-by-step procedure as far as **step 6**; see p. 58)

Step 2 Obtain $F = \dfrac{\text{larger variance}}{\text{smaller variance}}$

Step 3 Look up the significance of F in Table F. Note that you need two sets of degrees of freedom to do this. The columns in the table refer to the degrees of freedom of the top line of F ($N_1 = N_A - 1$, where N_A is the number of scores making up the larger variance). The rows in the table refer to the degrees of freedom of the bottom line of F ($N_2 = N_B - 1$, where N_B is the number of scores making up the smaller variance)

Step 4 Translate the results of the test back in terms of the experiment

Note The values in Table F are appropriate for a two-tail test (i.e. testing for a difference in the variances without _a priori_ specifying the direction of the difference). Many tables of F refer to a one-tail test, which is useful in a different application of F

Worked example

Variance-ratio test (*F*-test)

The following error scores were obtained in an aiming test
Non-preferred hand (A): 3·3, 2·1, 4·7, 0·1, 5·6, 0·0, 4·7
Preferred hand (B): 5·6, 4·9, 6·2, 5·1, 5·8, 6·3

Step 1 (using the method on p. 58)

X_A	(3a) X_A^2			X_B	(3a) X_B^2
3·3	10·89			5·6	31·36
2·1	4·41			4·9	24·01
4·7	22·09			6·2	38·44
0·1	0·01			5·1	26·01
5·6	31·36			5·8	33·64
0·0	0·00			6·3	39·69
4·7	22·09				

(1) $\Sigma X_A = 20\cdot5$ (3b) $\Sigma X_A^2 = 90\cdot85$ (1) $\Sigma X_B = 33\cdot9$ (3b) $\Sigma X_B^2 = 193\cdot15$

(2) $\overline{X}_A = \dfrac{20\cdot5}{7} = 2\cdot93$ $\qquad$ (2) $\overline{X}_B = \dfrac{33\cdot9}{6} = 5\cdot65$

(4a) $(\Sigma X_A)^2 = 20\cdot5^2 = 420\cdot25$ $\qquad$ (4a) $(\Sigma X_B)^2 = 33\cdot9^2 = 1149\cdot21$

(4b) $\dfrac{(\Sigma X_A)^2}{N_A} = \dfrac{420\cdot25}{7} = 60\cdot04$ $\qquad$ (4b) $\dfrac{(\Sigma X_B)^2}{N_B} = \dfrac{1149\cdot21}{6} = 191\cdot54$

(5) $\Sigma X_A^2 - \dfrac{(\Sigma X_A)^2}{N_A} = 90\cdot85 - 60\cdot04$ (5) $\Sigma X_B^2 - \dfrac{(\Sigma X_B)^2}{N_B} = 193\cdot15 - 191\cdot54$
$\qquad\qquad\qquad = 30\cdot81$ $\qquad\qquad\qquad\qquad\qquad = 1\cdot61$

(6) variance$_A = \dfrac{30\cdot81}{6} = \underline{5\cdot14}$ $\qquad$ (6) variance$_B = \dfrac{1\cdot61}{5} = \underline{0\cdot322}$

Step 2 $\quad F = \dfrac{5\cdot14}{0\cdot322} = 15\cdot9$

Step 3 $\quad N_1 = N_A - 1 = 6; \qquad N_2 = N_B - 1 = 5$
Table value of $F = 6\cdot98$ ($p = 0\cdot05$)
As the observed value of F exceeds the table value,
there is a significant difference between the variances at the
5 per cent level

Step 4 Inspection of the results shows that the variance for the
non-preferred hand exceeds that for the preferred hand.
This difference is significant at the 5 per cent level

6 Chi square

The chi-square techniques to be introduced in this chapter involve data in the form of **frequencies**. In other words, they deal with the situation where we are simply counting the number of times a *particular event occurs*. Suppose, for example, that a test is made of the effectiveness of a new teaching method, and the only information available is whether students pass or fail a test after the teaching experience. We would then be able to count the number of passes and of failures for the new method and for some appropriate control group.

Data in the form of measurements such as were used in the *t*-test described in the last chapter would not be appropriate for chi-square. However, it is possible to convert measures into counts by appropriate grouping so that chi-square is appropriate. For example, if heights of a group of subjects are available, these could be converted into counts of *tall* (say over 180 cm), *medium* (180 to 165 cm) and *short* (under 165 cm). Information is, of course, lost by this procedure, but it may be that the experimental hypothesis can still be adequately tested by the frequency data.

The 2 × 2 contingency table

In studying the possible relationship between smoking and cancer, the data of Table 8 were obtained (fictitious data, if it is any comfort for smokers). This is an example of a 2 × 2 contingency table – often referred to as a fourfold table. It shows in compact form that, of 1425 subjects investigated, 695 were smokers and 730 were non-smokers. Of the smokers, 230 had developed lung cancer by a certain age, 465 had not. Of the non-smokers, 78 had developed lung cancer and 652 had not. We want to know if smokers are more likely to get cancer. We can see, of course, that the *proportion* of smokers developing cancer in our sample is greater than the proportion of non-smokers developing cancer, but what we need to find out is how unlikely it is to get a difference in the proportions as large as is found here if in fact there is no difference between smokers and non-smokers in the population as a whole. We are talking here once more of 'sample' and 'population' in the statistical sense and we would have to be given detailed information as to how the subjects for the 'experiment' were chosen before we could make statements about the populations involved.

Table 8 Smokers and non-smokers having cancer or not having cancer (fictitious data)

	Smokers	Non-smokers	
cancer	230	78	308
no cancer	465	652	1117
	695	730	1425

The chi-square technique described in this chapter provides a test of the significance of the difference in proportions. It can be thought of in a rather different way – as a test of association between the categories used. That is, does membership of a given class on one dimension (e.g. smokers on the smoking/non-smoking dimension) tend to be associated with membership of a given class on the other dimension (e.g. cancer sufferers on the cancer/no-cancer dimension)?

If there is no association between the categories, the expected frequencies can be worked out for each of the four 'cells'. As 308 develop cancer out of a total of 1425 subjects (smokers and non-smokers), one would expect that the same proportion of smokers would develop cancer. Therefore, out of 692 smokers, a proportion of $\frac{308}{1425}$ would develop cancer, and the expected frequency E is

$$695 \times \frac{308}{1425} = 150 \cdot 3.$$

As 1117 out of 1425 overall do not develop the disease, one would expect this proportion of the 695 smokers to escape,

i.e. $\dfrac{695 \times 1117}{1425} = 544.7$.

Expected frequencies can be worked out in the same way for the other two cells. A general formula which can be used for computing expected frequencies is

$$E = \frac{\textbf{row total} \times \textbf{column total}}{\textbf{grand total}}$$

The table of expected frequencies is shown as Table 9.

Table 9 Expected frequencies calculated from the data of Table 8, on the basis of no association between the categories.

	Smokers	Non-smokers
cancer	150·3	157·7
no cancer	544.7	572.3

The chi-square statistic χ^2 can be computed from the observed O and expected E frequencies using the formula

chi square (for 2×2 table) $\chi^2 = \displaystyle\sum \frac{(|O - E| - \frac{1}{2})^2}{E}$,

where $|O - E|$ means 'find the absolute value of $O - E$', i.e. call the difference betwen O and E positive, both when E is smaller and when E is larger than O. The absolute value of this difference is then reduced by subtracting $\frac{1}{2}$, and the result is squared. This is then divided by the expected frequency for that cell. The sum of these values for each of the cells is χ^2. It can be seen that any discrepancy between O and E increases χ^2, and hence we accept that the IV is affecting the DV when χ^2 exceeds an appropriate value obtained from tables. In our example,

$$\text{observed } \chi^2 = \frac{(|230 - 150\cdot3| - 0\cdot5)^2}{150\cdot3} + \frac{(|78 - 157\cdot7| - 0\cdot5)^2}{157\cdot7}$$

$$+ \frac{(|465 - 544\cdot7| - 0\cdot5)^2}{544\cdot7} + \frac{(|652 - 572\cdot3| - 0\cdot5)^2}{572\cdot3}$$

$$= 41\cdot74 + 39\cdot76 + 11\cdot51 + 10\cdot96$$

$$= 103\cdot97.$$

This can be assessed for significance by using Table G. However, in order to use this table, one has to know the appropriate **degrees of freedom**.

Degrees of freedom

In obtaining the expected frequencies, the column and row totals (and hence the grand total) are taken as fixed. This means that when any *one* of the expected frequencies has been computed, the rest can be found by subtraction from the marginal totals. The implication of this is that a 2×2 table of this type has only one 'degree of freedom', i.e. only one of the frequencies can be considered as free to vary if we are to ensure that the marginal totals add up to the right value. Thus from Table G

$$\chi^2 = 3\cdot841$$

with 1 degree of freedom (1 d.f.), at the 5 per cent level.

We now go through the sub-routine which you should be familiar with from all the tests we have dealt with so far. As the observed χ^2 exceeds the table χ^2 for the 5 per cent level, we have evidence that the IV has affected the DV – specifically in this case that there is an association between the IV (smoking or not smoking) and the DV (incidence of cancer). Note that the table for χ^2 refers to the one-tailed test. This is appropriate for all the applications of χ^2 referred to in this chapter. We are concerned with just the upper tail of the chi-square distribution in all of these applications because large discrepancies between observed and expected frequencies, the significance of which we are trying to test, will be reflected in large values of χ^2, which would take us into the upper tail of the distribution.

The lower tail of the distribution corresponds to observed and expected frequencies being closer together than is likely on a chance basis, which is not usually of experimental interest.

You should note that this is a rather different issue from that covered in the discussion of one and two-tail t-tests (p. 80). There, the one-tail test was concerned with situations where we start out by predicting the direction of the difference between two conditions, and one needs to have a very good reason for using it instead of the two-tail test. With χ^2 the one-tail test is the norm and simply refers to large differences between observed and expected frequencies irrespective of the direction of the association.

Chi square and small samples

As the chi-square function is a continuous curve and the observed frequencies used in its estimation must take on whole number values, the actual sampling distribution is only approximated by the continuous function.

The formula for χ^2 given above incorporates **Yates's correction** – subtraction of $\frac{1}{2}$ from the absolute value of $(O - E)$ – which improves the approximation to a continuous function. It should be included for all cases of the use of χ^2 with 1 degree of freedom.

The smaller the sample size, the worse is the fit to a continuous distribution and below a certain size χ^2 should not be used. Although statisticians differ on the exact number below which χ^2 should not be used, a simple rule of thumb is: **do not use chi square if one or more of the** *expected* **frequencies falls below five**.

For the 2×2 table, an alternative small-sample test can be used called **Fisher's exact test**. This test can be found in more advanced texts, such as Siegel (1956).

Independence of observations

There are probably more inappropriate and incorrect uses of the chi-square statistic than of all other statistics put together. For one thing it can only be used appropriately if each and every observation is independent of each and every other observation. Violations of this rule are very common in the misuses of χ^2. As was pointed out previously, if we have more than a single observation from each subject, then it is unlikely that the observations are independent. In a situation where a subject has to make repeated choices between alternatives, it is likely that he will remember, or be otherwise influenced by, his earlier choices; the choices will, in other words, not be independent of each other.

In order to use χ^2 appropriately, each observation has to qualify for one and *only one* cell in the table. Another common misuse of the statistic occurs when an attempt is made to leave out some of the observations. For example, if one of the categorizations is in terms of success or failure on a task, some of the observations will be 'successes', others 'failures'. It would be incorrect to attempt to use the 'successes' alone – both successes and failures must go into the table.

Interpretation of the result of a chi-square test

A 'significant' χ^2 is evidence for an association. Inspection of the data given above shows that the direction of this association is such that smokers are more likely to get cancer. In this sample the proportion of smokers who get cancer is

$$\frac{230}{695} = 0.33.$$

The proportion of non-smokers who get cancer is

$$\frac{78}{730} = 0.11.$$

It is, of course, in attempting to interpret this result that we have to exercise caution. We are certainly not in a position to say 'smoking causes cancer'; however, there is an indication that the reason for this association is worth looking at. As is well known, the implication of a causal relationship here has been hotly disputed by many smokers and by cigarette manufacturers. One suggestion has been that people of a certain personality type are more likely to smoke *and also* have cancer. Put more generally, the argument is that there is a third factor (personality type) which is associated with both the others.

This example can stand as a warning of the difficulties in interpreting the results of a statistical test. These difficulties are by no means restricted to χ^2, but they often crop up in a particularly awkward form with this test. This reinforces the general argument put forward in the first chapter in favour of experimentation as opposed to other forms of observation. If we had been able to perform a proper experiment on smoking and cancer in humans, then we would be on much stronger ground. But this would have involved getting a random sample from the population and then allocating subjects randomly to smoking and non-smoking groups – that is, people would be told either that they must smoke or they must not smoke. You can probably anticipate the objections to such a procedure.

2 × 2 Chi square (test of association)

Use this test for *frequency data* only, i.e. for *counts* of different types of 'events'

Step 1 Draw up the 2 × 2 table, making sure that each event goes into one of the cells and into not more than one cell. The number in each cell is the **observed frequency** O for that cell

Step 2 Find the row totals, column totals and grand total

Step 3 Work out the **expected frequency** E for each cell separately using the formula

$$E = \frac{\text{row total} \times \text{column total}}{\text{grand total}}$$

Put the expected frequency for each cell into that cell

Worked example

2 × 2 Chi square (test of association)

A psychologist studying the symptoms of a random sample of 25 psychotics and 25 neurotics found that only 5 of the psychotics had suicidal feelings, whereas 12 of the neurotics had. Is there evidence for an association between the two psychiatric groups and the presence or absence of suicidal feelings?

Step 1

	Psychotics	*Neurotics*
suicidal	5	12
non-suicidal	20	13

Step 2

5	12	17
20	13	33
25	25	50

Step 3 For top left cell (cell A) $\quad E = \dfrac{17 \times 25}{50} = 8 \cdot 5$

For top right cell (cell B) $\quad E = \dfrac{17 \times 25}{50} = 8 \cdot 5$

For bottom left cell (cell C) $\quad E = \dfrac{33 \times 25}{50} = 16 \cdot 5$

For bottom right cell (cell D) $\quad E = \dfrac{33 \times 25}{50} = 16 \cdot 5$

8·5 5	8·5 12	17
16·5 20	16·5 13	33
25	25	50

2 × 2 Chi square (test of association)

Step 4 Work out the difference between O and E for each cell, taking the smaller of these from the larger in each case, i.e. obtain $|O - E|$

Step 5 Take away $\frac{1}{2}$ from $|O - E|$ for each cell $|O - E| - \frac{1}{2}$

Step 6 Square this for each cell $(|O - E| - \frac{1}{2})^2$

Step 7 Divide by the appropriate E value for that cell

$$\frac{(|O - E| - \frac{1}{2})^2}{E}$$

Step 8 Obtain χ^2 by adding all these contributions from the different cells

$$\chi^2 = \sum \frac{(|O - E| - \frac{1}{2})^2}{E}$$

This has 1 degree of freedom

Step 9 If the χ^2 obtained exceeds the table value (found in Table G) at the chosen level of significance, then there is evidence for an association between the categories

Step 10 Translate the result of the test back in terms of your experiment

Worked example – continued

2 × 2 Chi square (test of association)

	Step 4 $|O - E|$	Step 5 $|O - E| - \frac{1}{2}$
Cell A	$|5 - 8\cdot5| = 3\cdot5$	$3\cdot5 - 0\cdot5 = 3$
Cell B	$|12 - 8\cdot5| = 3\cdot5$	$3\cdot5 - 0\cdot5 = 3$
Cell C	$|20 - 16\cdot5| = 3\cdot5$	$3\cdot5 - 0\cdot5 = 3$
Cell D	$|13 - 16\cdot5| = 3\cdot5$	$3\cdot5 - 0\cdot5 = 3$

	Step 6 $(|O - E| - |\frac{1}{2}|)^2$	Step 7 $\dfrac{(|O - E| - \frac{1}{2})^2}{E}$
Cell A	$3^2 = 9$	$9/8\cdot5 = 1\cdot0588$
Cell B	$3^2 = 9$	$9/8\cdot5 = 1\cdot0588$
Cell C	$3^2 = 9$	$9/16\cdot5 = 0\cdot5454$
Cell D	$3^2 = 9$	$9/16\cdot5 = 0\cdot5454$

Step 8
$$\chi^2 = \sum \frac{(|O - E| - \frac{1}{2})^2}{E}$$
$$= 1\cdot0588 + 1\cdot0588 + 0\cdot5454 + 0\cdot5454$$
$$= 3\cdot2084$$
$$= 3\cdot21 \text{ with 1 d.f.}$$

Step 9 From Table G,
$\chi^2 = 3\cdot84$
with 1 d.f., at the 5 per cent significance level

Step 10 There is not significant evidence for an association between psychotism/neuroticism and presence/absence of suicidal feelings at the conventional (5 per cent) significance level (or *alternatively*, the proportion of psychotics with suicidal feelings does not differ significantly from the proportion of neurotics with suicidal feelings)

Chi-square in larger tables

Chi-square can be used in tables with more than two rows and more than two columns. Once again it can be regarded as a test of association between the attributes which make up the rows and those which make up the columns. The formula is then simplified, as Yates's correction is not needed.

thus $\chi^2 = \sum \dfrac{(O - E)^2}{E}$

the summation sign indicating that the quantities $(O - E)^2/E$, having been computed for each cell, should be added together for all the cells.

The calculation of expected frequencies is as for the 2×2 table

i.e. $E = \dfrac{\text{row total} \times \text{column total}}{\text{grand total}}$,

the reasoning behind this being exactly the same as for the 2×2 case.

The number of degrees of freedom can also be arrived at as in the 2×2 case. If the row totals are considered fixed, then the frequency in one cell in any row is fixed when values have been given to the frequencies of the other cells. The same applies to the columns, so that in a table with R rows and C columns, the total number of degrees of freedom is

$(R - 1) \times (C - 1)$.

This is perhaps clearer when displayed; Figure 18 shows it for a 3×4 table and a 2×6 table. When values have been given to the frequencies of the unshaded cells then, given fixed marginal totals, the values of frequencies for each of the shaded cells can be computed:

for the 3×4 table
degrees of freedom = $(3 - 1) \times (4 - 1) = 6$

and for the 2×6 table
degrees of freedom = $(2 - 1) \times (6 - 1) = 5$.

3 × 4 table

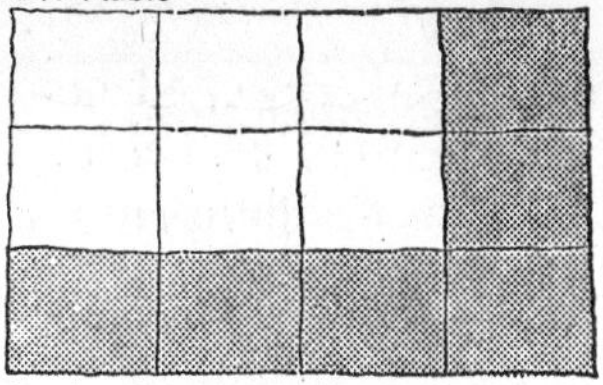

2 × 3 = 6 degrees of freedom

2 × 6 table

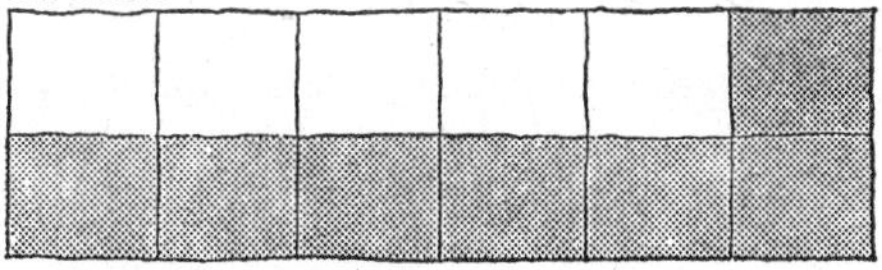

1 × 5 = 5 degrees of freedom

Figure 18 Degrees of freedom in large χ^2 tables

In interpreting larger tables it may be helpful to convert the observed cell frequencies into proportions. Table 10 shows this for the data in the worked example on p. 109.

Table 10 Contingency table with observed frequencies expressed as proportions

	Method A	*Method B*	*Method C*	*Overall*
pass	$\frac{50}{55} = 0.91$	$\frac{42}{61} = 0.69$	$\frac{56}{64} = 0.88$	$\frac{148}{180} = 0.82$
fail	$\frac{5}{55} = 0.09$	$\frac{19}{61} = 0.31$	$\frac{8}{64} = 0.13$	$\frac{32}{180} = 0.18$

However, while it is often easier to pick out what is happening from the proportions, remember that χ^2 must be calculated from the frequencies themselves.

Step-by-step procedure

Chi-square – tables larger than 2 × 2 (test of association)

Use this test for *frequency data* only, i.e. for *counts* of different types of 'events'

Step 1 Draw up the table, making sure that each event goes into one of the cells and into no more than one cell. The number in each cell is the **observed frequency O** for that cell

Step 2 Find the row totals, column totals and grand total

Step 3 Work out the **expected frequency E** for each cell separately using the formula

$$E = \frac{\text{row total} \times \text{column total}}{\text{grand total}}$$

Put the expected frequency for each cell into that cell

Worked example

Chi square – tables larger than 2 × 2 (test of association)

In an exam, varying numbers of students passed and failed after having been taught by one of three different methods. It is required to test for an association between the numbers passing and failing and the method of instruction (i.e. does the relative proportion of passes differ from method to method?)

Step 1

	Method A	Method B	Method C
pass	50	42	56
fail	5	19	8

Step 2

50	42	56	148
5	19	8	32
55	61	64	180

Step 3 For top left-hand cell,

$$E = \frac{148 \times 55}{180} = 45 \cdot 22$$

and so on for each of the cells:

45·22 50	50·16 42	52·62 56	148
9·78 5	10·84 19	11·38 8	32
55	61	64	180

Chi-square – tables larger than 2 × 2 (test of association)

Step 4 Work out $(O - E)$ for each cell

Step 5 Square this for each cell

Step 6 Divide by the appropriate E value for that cell

Step 7 Obtain χ^2 by adding all these contributions from the different cells

Step 8 Obtain the degrees of freedom =
(number of rows − 1) × (number of columns − 1)

Step 9 If the χ^2 obtained exceeds the table value (found in Table G) at the chosen level of significance, then there is evidence for an association between the categories

Step 10 Translate the result of the test back in terms of the experiment

Worked example – continued

Chi-square – tables larger than 2 × 2 (test of association)

O	E	Step 4 $(O - E)$	Step 5 $(O - E)^2$	Step 6 $(O - E)^2_E$
50	45·22	4·78	22·85	0·505
42	50·16	−8·16	66·59	1·328
56	52·62	3·38	11·42	0·217
5	9·78	−4·78	22·85	2·336
19	10·84	8·16	66·59	6·143
8	11·38	−3·38	11·42	1·004

Step 7 $\chi^2 = \sum \dfrac{(O - E)^2}{E}$

$$= 0·505 + 1·328 + 0·217 + 2·336 + 6·143 + 1·004$$
$$= 11·53$$

Step 8 d.f. = (rows − 1) × (columns − 1) = 1 × 2 = 2

Step 9 From Table G, $\chi^2 = 5·99$ with 2 d.f. at the 5 per cent significance level. As the χ^2 obtained (11·53) is greater than this table value, there is significant evidence for an association between the variables

Step 10 There is significant evidence for an association between method of instruction and relative proportion of passes. In other words, the relative proportions of passes differ significantly from one method to another

Note That the significance applies to the data taken as a whole. However inspection of the table suggests that it is Method B which differs from the other two

Small samples in larger tables

Yates's correction is inappropriate for χ^2 with more than one degree of freedom, and its disappearance from the formula has been noted. It is recommended that the same rule of thumb be applied as for small samples: **do not use chi square if one or more of the expected frequencies falls below five**.

This is a conservative procedure in that circumstances may arise when the approximation to the chi-square distribution is adequate with smaller expected frequencies than this.

A common expedient when small expected frequencies are obtained is to pool categories in order to get total frequencies above the magic number of five. There are great difficulties in doing this, however. Possibly the hypothesis that one is interested in testing cannot be tested if categories are lumped together in this way. And even if this is still possible, a *post hoc* pooling (i.e. after the observed frequencies have been obtained) will affect the randomness of the sample. Although exact tests exist as for the 2 × 2 case, they are difficult to compute. The obvious procedure to adopt is to take a large enough sample for the expected frequencies to be over five. If appropriate, categories can be combined in *a priori* fashion (i.e. before collecting the results). Finally, if one does end up with some low expected frequencies then it is probably preferable to go ahead with χ^2 adding a caveat that there may be a relatively poor approximation to the exact probabilities.

Chi square as a test of goodness of fit

We have so far considered χ^2 as a test of association, where the expected frequencies can be calculated directly from the observed frequencies by assuming independence between the categories. It is also possible to use χ^2 in a rather different way where the expected frequencies are obtained from predictions based on theoretical considerations. When the χ^2 statistic is computed in this way, it becomes a test of the **goodness of fit** between the observations and the theory.

Chi square can, for instance, be used to determine whether a given set of data may be regarded as a sample from a normal population, and also to decide whether or not a particular statistical test which assumes a normal distribution could be validly used in some situation.

We will restrict ourselves in this chapter to a simple case which occurs quite frequently. This is where, in a single-row χ^2, we are testing the hypothesis of equal probability of occurrence of the different alternatives (this is equivalent to testing the goodness of fit to a **rectangular distribution**). Thus the expected frequency for each cell is obtained simply by dividing the total number of observations by the number of cells in the row. Degrees of freedom are one less than the number of cells, the reasoning being as before. The formula used is unchanged, and Yates's correction should be employed in the one degree of freedom case. The same rule of thumb for expected frequencies applies.

1 × N Chi square (test of goodness of fit)

Use this test for *frequency data* only, i.e. for *counts* of different types of 'events'

Step 1 Draw up the 1 × N table, making sure that each event goes into one of the cells and into not more than one cell. The number in each cell is the **observed frequency** O for that cell

Step 2 Find the **total frequency**

Step 3 Work out the **expected frequency** E for each cell separately, using the theoretical distribution to be fitted. For the special case of the rectangular distribution we are considering, there is an equal probability of occurrence of the different alternatives.

$$E = \frac{\text{total frequency}}{N} \text{ for each cell}$$

Worked example

1 × N Chi square (test of goodness of fit)

A sample of 250 people in the street were asked to 'say any number from 0 to 9 inclusive'. Do the results show any evidence for number preference?

Step 1	Digit	Observed frequency
	0	18
	1	31
	2	29
	3	36
	4	17
	5	20
	6	20
	7	35
	8	14
	9	30

Step 2 Total frequency = 250

Step 3 In the absence of number preference, all observed frequencies will have the same expected value

i.e. $E = \dfrac{250}{10} = 25$

Step-by-step procedure – continued

1 × N Chi square (test of goodness of fit)

Step 4 Work out $(O - E)$ for each cell
NB for the 1 d.f. case, Yates's correction must be applied, i.e. take $(|O - E| - \frac{1}{2})$ for each cell

Step 5 Square this for each cell

Step 6 Divide by E

Step 7 Obtain χ^2 by adding all these contributions from the different cells

Step 8 Obtain the degrees of freedom = (number of cells − 1)

Step 9 If the χ^2 obtained exceeds the value found in Table G at the chosen level of significance, then there is evidence for a divergence between the theoretical and observed distributions

Step 10 Translate the result of the test back in terms of the experiment

1 × N Chi square (test of goodness of fit)

O	E	Step 4 $(O - E)$	Step 5 $(O - E)^2$	Step 6 $(O - E)^2/E$
18	25	−7	49	1·96
31	25	6	36	1·44
29	25	4	16	0·64
36	25	11	121	4·84
17	25	−8	64	2·56
20	25	−5	25	1·00
20	25	−5	25	1·00
35	25	10	100	4·00
14	25	−11	121	4·84
30	25	5	25	1·00

Step 7 $\chi^2 = \sum \dfrac{(O - E)^2}{E} = 1·96 + 1·44 + 0·64 + 4·84 +$
$+ 2·56 + 1·00 + 1·00 + 4·00 +$
$+ 4·84 + 1·00$
$= 23·28$

Step 8   d.f. = (number of cells − 1) = 9

Step 9   From Table G, $\chi^2 = 16·92$ at the 5 per cent significance level with 9 d.f. As the observed χ^2 exceeds the table χ^2 at the 5 per cent level, there is evidence for a significant departure from equal choices of the different digits

Step 10 The results of the experiment show significant evidence for number preferences

7 Parametric and non-parametric tests

Parametric tests

As discussed in Chapter 5, the t-test and the variance-ratio test make certain assumptions about the underlying population distributions. Because of this, such tests are often called 'parametric', as their derivation involves assumptions about the 'parameters' of population distribution ('parameters' are simply measures computed from all the observations in a population – examples are the population mean and standard deviation. We often use statistics, that is measures computed from a *sample*, in order to estimate parameters).

Such tests are often *robust* (What is robust? See p. 79), but there are obviously some situations, particularly in the case of small samples, where it is unreasonable to make the assumptions, which brings us to the Mann-Whitney and Wilcoxon tests.

The Mann-Whitney and Wilcoxon tests

There are tests which are much less dependent on population distributions and parameters than those so far considered. In this chapter we will consider two tests, the Mann-Whitney and Wilcoxon tests, which do a very similar job to the uncorrelated and correlated t-tests respectively. Whilst they are commonly called *non*-parametric tests, it should not be thought that they are completely free of any assumptions. Certainly an experiment which is to be analysed using a non-parametric technique needs just as careful attention to points of experimental design, randomization, etc., as does one to be analysed using a parametric technique. The tests to be described are sometimes called 'order techniques', that is, they are based on orderings or rankings of the data. Suppose that a subject is asked to rank in order of preference eight foods, four of which are savoury and four sweet. If the subject ranks the four sweet foods as first, second, third and fourth, then it would appear likely that he prefers sweet foods to savoury foods. The mathematical basis for this is straightforward. If we had the names of the foods written on cards and shuffled thoroughly, then what would be the chances that the four 'sweet' cards would be turned over first? This probability can be calculated quite simply, and is pretty low. This randomization of all possible orderings forms the basis of the Mann-Whitney and Wilcoxon tests. The data can be in the form of rankings, as discussed above, or actual measures can be taken which are then converted into ranks.

Before discussing the tests in detail, a couple of points ought to be made. Firstly, the non-parametric test does not normally test exactly the same thing as the corresponding parametric test. Effectively, the general procedure is the same as in the food example just considered. We start with the hypothesis that each of the orders in which the set of eight cards might be turned over is equally likely to occur. If the IV has no effect on the DV, this will be the case. Then, as in other tests, if the results obtained in an actual experiment are highly improbable given that the above hypothesis is true, we come to the decision that the IV does affect the DV. Another way of putting the distinction between what the parametric and non-parametric tests actually test is to say that, whereas the t-test tests for a specific difference in the means of the population, the corresponding non-parametric test is a general test of whether or not the populations are the same.

A second point is that in situations where both types of test are appropriate, the **power efficiency** of the non-parametric test is lower than its parametric counterpart. This means that, in general, it is less sensitive at detecting an effect of the independent variable on the dependent variable. To detect any given effect at a specified significance level, a larger sample size is required for the non-parametric test than the parametric test. This is expressed as

power efficiency of test A compared with test B $= \dfrac{N_B}{N_A} \times 100,$

where N_A is the sample size needed to show a significant effect at the 5 per cent level for test A, and N_B the sample size needed to show a significant effect at the 5 per cent level for test B.

Mann-Whitney test

This is the non-parametric counterpart of the uncorrelated t-test for equality of means. It can be used with independent-subjects designs.

A step-by-step procedure and worked example are given for the small-sample case, with instructions for dealing with larger samples.

Step-by-step procedure

Mann-Whitney test – small-sample* case

For **independent-subjects designs:** use instead of uncorrelated t-test if data is either (a) in the form of ranks or (b) obviously non-normal or (c) there is an obvious difference in the variance of the two groups

Step 1 Rank data (taking both groups together) giving rank 1 to the lowest score, and so on

Step 2 Find the sum of the ranks for the smaller sample – A in the example opposite – (if both samples are the same size, find the sum of ranks of sample A). Call this T

Step 3 Find $U = N_A N_B + \dfrac{N_A (N_A + 1)}{2} - T$,

where N_A is the number of scores in the smaller sample (or, if both samples are the same size, the sample whose ranks were totalled to find T)

Step 4 Find $U' = N_A N_B - U$

Step 5 Look up the *smaller* of U and U' in Table H. There is a significant difference if the observed value is equal to or less than the table value

Step 6 Translate the result of the test back in terms of the experiment

Treatment of ties

Give the mean rank to the tied observations. Thus, if 2 scores of 10 tie for 5th and 6th ranks, give each score a rank of 5·5. If 3 scores of 18 tie for 12th, 13th and 14th ranks, give each score a rank of 13. The test should not be used if there is a large proportion of ties.

*Not more than 20 observations in either set of scores

Worked example

Mann-Whitney test – small-sample case

Solution times of anagrams under condition A (single category) or condition B (multiple categories) were as follows:

A	B	Step 1	A	B
3	23		1	5
5	37		2	7
97	64		9	8
12	24		3	6
	14			4

Step 2 $T = 1 + 2 + 9 + 3 = 15$

Step 3 $N_A = 4$, $\quad N_B = 5$

$$U = (4 \times 5) + \frac{(4 \times 5)}{2} - 15$$

$$= 15$$

Step 4 $U' = (4 \times 5) - U$
$$= 20 - 15$$
$$= 5$$

Step 5 As U' is less than U, look up U' in Table H. Table value for $N_A = 4$, $N_B = 5$ is 1. The observed value (5) is not equal to or less than the table value, therefore there is not significant evidence that the scores under the two conditions differ

Step 6 Anagram solution times under the two conditions (single and multiple categories) do not differ significantly

Mann-Whitney test – large-sample case

The sampling distribution of U approaches the normal distribution when the sample size becomes large. We will take as 'large' samples those in which the larger of the two samples has 20 or more observations. The procedure is to obtain U as in the small-sample case (steps 1–3 inclusive). The standard deviation of U can then be found as

$$SD_U = \sqrt{\frac{N_A N_B (N_A + N_B + 1)}{12}}$$

and a z-score (see p. 60) as

$$z = \left(U - \frac{N_A N_B}{2} \right) \div SD_U.$$

If we are dealing with a two-tailed test, then the observed z is significant at the 5 per cent level if it exceeds 1·96. For a one-tailed test, 5 per cent significance is attained if z exceeds 1·64 (check these in Table D if you are in doubt).

The ranking procedure can become quite laborious with large samples. Partly for this reason and partly because violations of the assumptions behind parametric statistics become less important for large samples, the Mann-Whitney test tends to be restricted to use with small samples.

The Wilcoxon test

This is the non-parametric counterpart to the correlated t-test for equality of means. It is suitable for use with the matched-subjects or repeated-measures designs. We have already considered a non-parametric test which is appropriate for use in this design (the sign test p. 45).

The Wilcoxon test is intermediate between the sign test and the correlated t-test in the amount of information which is extracted from the data. In the sign test, we only take into account the sign of the difference between each pair of scores; in the t-test, the actual size of the difference is used in computation. In the Wilcoxon test, one uses the sign of the difference and additionally *orders* the sizes of these differences.

As one might expect, the sign test is low in power efficiency (what is power efficiency? See p. 119), the Wilcoxon test intermediate and the correlated *t*-test most efficient. However, there is in fact only a small difference in the power efficiencies of Wilcoxon and correlated *t*-tests in situations where either could be used.

The Wilcoxon test is similar both in rationale and in computation to the Mann-Whitney test.

Step-by-step procedure

Wilcoxon test – small-sample* case

For matched-subjects or repeated-measures designs: use instead of a correlated t-test if either (a) the differences between treatments can only be ranked in size or (b) the data is obviously non-normal or (c) there is an obvious difference in the variance of the two groups

Step 1 Obtain the difference between each pair of readings, taking sign into account

Step 2 Rank order these differences (ignoring the sign), giving rank 1 to the smallest difference

Step 3 Obtain T, the sum of the ranks for differences with the less frequent sign

Step 4 Consult Table J. If the observed T is equal to or less than the table value, then there is a significant difference between the two conditions

Step 5 Translate the result of the test back in terms of the experiment

*Not more than 8 pairs of scores

Worked example

Wilcoxon – small-sample case

Eight pairs of twins were tested in complex reaction time
situations; one member of each pair was tested after drinking
3 double whiskies, the other member was completely sober.
The following reaction times were recorded:

Sober group	Whisky group	Step 1 Differences	Step 2 Ranks
310	300	−10	1
340	320	−20	2
290	360	70	5
270	320	50	4
370	540	170	6
330	360	30	3
320	680	360	7
320	1120	800	8

Step 3 Less frequent sign of difference is negative,
$T = 1 + 2 = 3$

Step 4 From Table J, when $N = 8$, $T = 4$. As the observed value of
T is less than the table value, there is a significant
difference between the two conditions

Step 5 Complex reaction time scores are significantly higher after
drinking 3 double whiskies than when sober

Wilcoxon test – large-sample case

As with the Mann-Whitney test, the sampling distribution of the statistic (in this case T) approaches the normal distribution as the sample size becomes large. We will take large as meaning more than 8 pairs of scores. Having obtained T as in the small-sample case (**Steps 1–3** inclusive), the standard deviation of T is found as

$$SD_T = \sqrt{\frac{N(N + 1)(2N + 1)}{24}}$$

and a z-score as

$$z = \left\{ T - \frac{N(N + 1)}{4} \right\} \div SD_T.$$

The significance decisions are identical to those for the Mann-Whitney large-sample case. Thus, if we have a two-tailed test, the observed z is significant at the 5 per cent level if it exceeds 1.96. For the one-tailed test, significance is attained if z exceeds 1.64. However, as with the Mann-Whitney test, and for the same reasons, the Wilcoxon test tends to be restricted to use with small samples.

Comparison of Mann-Whitney and Wilcoxon tests with t-test

The power efficiency of the Mann-Whitney and Wilcoxon tests, whilst usually somewhat lower than the corresponding t-test, compares very favourably with it. The Mann-Whitney and Wilcoxon tests can be used in situations where the t-test would be inappropriate (e.g. where the assumptions of the t-test obviously do not apply). In other words, they are capable of wider application.

Different statisticians give different advice as to the relative merits of parametric and non-parametric tests. The non-parametric camp claim that their tests are simpler to compute, have less assumptions and can be used more widely. The parametric camp claim that their tests are robust with respect to violations of their assumptions and have greater power efficiency.

The strategy recommended here is to use the t-test *unless* the data is in the form of ranks, *or* where the sample is small, and either the distribution is obviously non-normal or there are obviously large differences in variance.

However, if you are particularly pressed for time or have a large number of analyses to do there is nothing particularly wicked or inappropriate about using non-parametric statistics even in cases where *t*-tests might have been used.

8 Interrelationship of design and analysis

In Chapter 2 we went through an example which illustrated the steps which have to be taken in designing an experiment. To recap, these were as follows:

Given that you have a problem (what is sometimes called a behavioural hypothesis), the first step is to turn it into a form which is capable of being tested experimentally. This means deciding on the **independent variable** and on the **dependent variable**. It means putting each of these variables into an operational form. You have also to decide how many levels of the independent variable you are going to use (i.e. how *many* experimental conditions or treatments). Remember that the techniques presented in this book deal directly only with the comparison of two treatments.

The next decision concerns how subjects fit into the experiment. This gives us our three basic experimental designs – **independent subjects, matched subjects** and **repeated measures**. Then you must decide on how many subjects, which will obviously be influenced by many things: how difficult they are to get, how long you can spend with each, and so on.

The kind of behavioural hypothesis that you start with, coupled with the experimental design, effectively decides for you the statistical test which you use. Relying solely on the techniques that are described in this book, there are very many experimental designs whose results you can evaluate statistically. Of course, there are many designs for which you have not been given the appropriate statistical techniques. This means that you cannot go blindly in and conduct an experiment without considering the way in which it is to be analysed. *The decisions about the statistics to be used must be made as a part of the design process.*

This is always true, no matter how sophisticated an arsenal of statistical techniques is at your disposal. It is only in cases where the experimenter has supreme confidence that he can demonstrate the effects of the independent variable completely unequivocally (as happens for instance in some cases with the application of Skinnerian methods and techniques) that statistical analysis may be unnecessary.

How to increase the sensitivity of the experiment

Many new experimenters get very discouraged by a string of non-significant results. It may well be that these are true cases where the independent variable has no effect on the dependent variable. Somebody new to the game of experimenting is likely to be unskilled in selecting the problems and situations where the variables *do* have an effect. On the other hand, it may be that an effect is there but, for one reason or another, the fledgling experimenter cannot detect it. There are many factors which could be playing a part here, and we will go through some of them in an attempt to show some of the ways in which an experiment may be made more sensitive at detecting experimental effects.

1 Reduce the 'noise' level

By this, I do not mean just the physical sound level but what is picturesquely called 'noise' – the effects of uncontrolled variables. These effects appear in many ways, for instance in the instructions given to subjects. If instructions vary slightly from subject to subject, then the scores obtained by the subjects might vary according to these instructions. If there is poor experimental control over the general conditions in the laboratory or wherever the experiment takes place (e.g. people talking or laughing, to which the subjects may sometimes pay attention and sometimes not), if the subjects are bored with the experiment or are more interested in interacting with the experimenter than with the experiment – these are all ways in which the scores might be expected to vary in ways which have nothing to do with the experimental variable being manipulated.

Now there is a good case for only being concerned with experimental effects which are sufficiently strong to show themselves in relatively naturalistic situations, but obviously the line must be drawn somewhere and the 'noise' must be kept down to a level at which the experimental effects have a chance to come through.

So lesson one is that the sensitivity of an experiment can be increased by *increasing the degree of experimental control* over the conditions under which the experiment takes place. Given that we have refined our procedures as much as possible, what else can be done?

2 More subjects

A second possibility is to increase the *sample size* – that is, the number of subjects taking part in the experiment. This makes the experiment more sensitive because the effect of the experimental variable (assuming that there is an effect) will add together over subjects, whereas the random error effects of the kind we have considered (which we will never be able to get rid of completely) will tend to cancel each other out as some will be in one direction, some in the other.

3 Floor and ceiling effects

A third thing to take into account is the *avoidance of possible 'floor' and 'ceiling' effects*. Another way of putting this is that the level of difficulty of the experimental situation should be adjusted so that the scores lie in the mid-range of the scale used. Thus, in a memory experiment, one might find that all the subjects score between 90 and 100 per cent correct and, consequently, any difference between experimental conditions would be reduced simply because the results of some subjects are bumping on the ceiling and hence not going as high as they would otherwise. The converse occurs if the material is too difficult and floor effects result.

The solution to this particular problem lies in careful pilot work to establish the kind of scores obtained in the experimental situation.

4 Increasing reliability of the measure

Another way in which the sensitivity can be increased is by *increasing the reliability of an individual measure*. The easiest way in which this can be done in psychological experimentation is by basing the measure not on a single observation but on a series of observations (e.g. using the mean). Thus any special effect unconnected with the experimental effect, say a loud noise just before an observation is made, might influence a single observation a great deal, but would have much less effect on the mean score. One has to consider carefully, of course, whether the experiment is such that taking a series of observations from a single subject is possible. In doing that, we are assuming that the observations are independent of each other, that they are all measures of the same thing. The reasonableness of this assumption varies very much from one experimental situation to another.

5 Which design?

Finally, one should consider the *relative sensitivity of the independent-subjects, matched-subjects and repeated-measures designs*. Generally, the sensitivity increases as one goes from independent subjects to matched subjects to repeated measures. This is due to the increasing degree of control over the variables associated with subjects. Thus in a repeated-measures design it is the same subject who appears under both conditions. In so far as scores under the experimental conditions may be affected by such things as age, sex, intelligence, personality, characteristics, etc., we obviously have perfect matching, and hence control over these variables, when it is the same subject under both conditions. With the matched-subjects design we retain some matching, but this is usually done on just a single variable. Hence the degree of matching is less than with repeated measures and the efficiency of the design will depend on how close a correlation exists between the matching variable and the dependent variable. If there is a high correlation, then the matching will be very effective. There is great difficulty, of course, in discovering high correlations of this kind.

With independent-subjects designs there is no attempt at all at matching, and therefore this design is least sensitive.

However, this should not be taken as an indication that we always aim for repeated-measures designs and avoid independent-subjects designs. The great weakness of repeated-measures designs lies simply in the fact that they do have repeated measures. Because a subject has to perform under *both* experimental conditions, there are all kinds of nasty effects which might occur.

One of the special peculiarities of humans is the extent to which they are learning animals – that is, the extent to which present behaviour is modified by past experiences. Thus, if we test the same person under two conditions, the result of the second condition tested will in very many cases be modified by the experience on the first condition tested. Whilst counter-balancing or randomization of the order of presentation of the two conditions can and should be used, it will only completely neutralize an order effect when this consists of a simple additive difference between the first and second conditions, irrespective of which conditions are first and second, and there is no guarantee that the effects will be as simple as this.

Thus the repeated-measures design is best used in situations where the learning effect is known to be small or negligible – for example in simple motor tasks without knowledge of results. Alternatively, if the inter-subject variability on a dependent variable is very high (so that an independent-subjects design would be unlikely to yield any results), one might be tempted to use a repeated-measures design.

If it is possible to convert an independent-subjects design into a matched-subjects design, then, providing that some meaningful way of matching can be devised (i.e. a matching variable which is known to correlate reasonably highly with performance on the dependent variable), the only disadvantage is the labour involved in getting the scores on the matching variable to make up the pairs of subjects.

Hence the strategy suggested is that of using a matched-subjects design if there is reasonably readily available a matching variable which correlates highly with the dependent variable. If this is not available, then a choice between independent-subjects and repeated-measures designs depends upon the likelihood that repeated measures would be independent. If this appears unlikely, then the independent-subjects design should be used.

More complex designs

Some indications of the kinds of ways in which the basic experimental designs can be complicated will now be considered.

More than two experimental conditions

Whilst it is possible to use our two-condition experimental design in order to test for the effect of the independent variable, there are several defects to this simple design. It may happen, for instance, that the two values of the independent variable which we have chosen happen not to show any effects, whereas the choice of two other values might have shown an effect. The obvious way of getting over this difficulty is to include a larger number of experimental conditions and to look for differences between these conditions. It is possible to use the t-test (or its non-parametric equivalents where appropriate) to look at conditions in pairs, but there are difficulties connected with significance level if this is done. Do not forget that a 5 per cent significance level means that there is a 5 per cent chance of deciding that the IV is affecting the DV when this is not the case. So, if one made 20 comparisons between pairs of conditions, one would expect 1 of these 20 (i.e. 5 out of 100 – 5 per cent) to come up with a significant effect even when there is no actual effect of IV on DV. Similarly, if one just looks at the results after they have been obtained, and picks out, say, the conditions with lowest and highest means, one is effectively going through all the other tests implicitly and the difficulties with significance level remain even though one might only compute a single t-test.

A second criticism of experiments with only two experimental conditions is that, whereas they can indicate whether or not an independent variable has an effect on a dependent variable, they cannot tell us anything of the nature of the functional relationship between the two variables.

Figure 19 shows three possibilities which would fit in with the same results on conditions A and B. The only way in which the nature of these relationships can be made clear is by including in the same experiment several values on the independent variable, so that more points can be filled in on the graph.

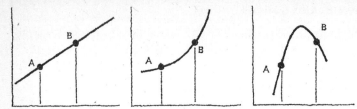

Figure 19 Three different relationships between independent and dependent variables consistent with known values at A and B

A technique which is useful for these designs is the **analysis of variance**, which is not covered in this text but is covered in detail in most advanced texts of psychological statistics.

More than one independent variable

There is no reason why an experiment need be limited to a single independent variable. This approach can be extended to three, four or as many variables as you wish. Designs with all possible combinations of levels of the different variables are called **factorial** designs. Their great advantage is that they can tell us about the effect of a single variable, not just when all other variables are held constant (as in the single variable design), but over a range of values of one or more other variables. Thus there is a greater generality to results.

A great advantage of factorial designs is that they bring out possible **interactions** between variables. An interaction occurs when the effect of one variable is not constant, but varies according to the level of another variable.

Let us suppose that a number of children were assessed on their degree of initiative on the one hand, and extent of parental encouragement on the other. Four groups of children were formed: low parental encouragement with low initiative, low parental encouragement with high initiative, high parental encouragement with low initiative and high parental encouragement with high initiative. Subsequent intelligence tests might have given the results shown graphically in Figure 20. There was an interaction between the two variables – parental encouragement and initiative – in the sense that, for children with low parental encouragement, it made

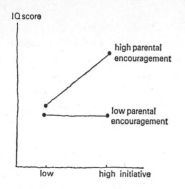

IQ score

high parental
encouragement

low parental
encouragement

low   high initiative

Figure 20 Interaction between the variables
of parental encouragement and initiative

little or no difference whether they had low or high initiative but, for
children with high parental encouragement, those with high initiative scored considerably higher than those with low initiative.

If one were trying to interpret these (fictitious) results, one would
have to bear in mind that this study was a survey rather than an
experiment. There are all the usual warnings (see Chapter 1) against
inferring causative relationships when one is not dealing with an
experiment.

Designs involving more than one independent variable cannot be
analysed directly by the techniques covered in this text. What is
required is the analysis of variance referred to in the previous
section. Otherwise, all that can be done is to perform separate
analyses of, in our example, the effect of parental encouragement
on high-initiative children and then the effect of parental encouragement on low-initiative children (e.g. a t-test in each case).

Alternatively, or additionally, one could perform similar tests on
the effect of initiative on the group with low parental encouragement and then the effect of initiative on the group with high parental
encouragement.

Whilst these tests can provide some kind of analysis of the data,
they do not tell us anything about possible interactions, and they are
really no adequate substitute for a full analysis.

More than one dependent variable

Just as it is possible to make use of more than one independent variable, so it is possible to have more than one dependent variable. Thus, there might be advantages in looking at the effect of our independent variable(s) on a whole range of other variables. If we are investigating the effects of sleep deprivation, it might appear sensible to use a whole battery of different testing situations, some cognitive, some perceptual, and so on.

If it is necessary to evaluate more than one dependent variable simultaneously, then so-called 'multivariate' procedures should be used. Most of these procedures are extremely complicated or tedious and cannot reasonably be carried out without using a digital computer. However, designs using a single dependent variable can be applied appropriately to most research problems because it is not usually possible to measure more than two or three dependent variables (which could be taken one by one if necessary) and quite often it is found that those variables that can be measured are highly correlated, so that any of them would be as useful as any other.

9 Carrying out the experiment and writing it up

Carrying out the experiment

Once you have designed your experiment, the next stage involves actually getting to grips with your subjects, as it were. The essential thing here is that you know exactly what you are going to do before you attempt to do it. There are a number of things that will help you to do this.

(1) Have verbatim (word-for-word) instructions for your subjects.

(2) Have a prepared work sheet which shows you clearly what you have to do and the order in which you have to do it. It should also have spaces into which you can fit the results as you get them. Figure 21 shows an example of a work sheet.

(3) If you have apparatus, make sure it works and that you know what to do with it for it to perform appropriately.

(4) If this is a laboratory-type experiment, make sure that your subject is adequately screened from (a) you as experimenter, together with your work sheet and any other information which should not be available to the subject, (b) other subjects and experimenters and the world at large. Obviously, sound-proofed cubicles are a great help in many experimental situations, but common sense can remove a lot of the possible interference and distraction from your subjects, e.g. using visual presentation of material and a visual metronome (light flashing at intervals) for pacing either presentation of material or response, rather than using auditory presentation.

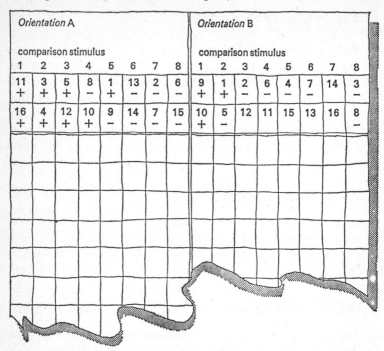

Figure 21 An example of a worksheet.
Sixteen trials have been presented under orientation A, the randomized order of presentation being indicated by the numbers in the cell. These are followed by 16 trials under orientation B, 10 of which have been presented – comparison stimulus 4 would be presented next. There would be 64 trials under each condition, counterbalanced according to the sequence ABAB–BABA (in blocks of 16). The 'scores' are simply + or –, indicating a judgement of 'greater than' or 'less than'

(5) **Most important of all**, have adequate pilot trials before you start the experiment proper. This ensures that the instructions are intelligible to the subjects and that they can perform appropriately in the situation. It helps you avoid 'floor' or 'ceiling' effects (what are floor and ceiling effects? See p. 132) by adjusting the difficulty of the

material depending on how the pilot subjects perform. You will find out as experimenter whether the task you have set yourself is feasible, e.g. whether you have enough time to make the appropriate manipulations and write down the results of one trial before the next is due, and so on. Quite often the inexperienced experimenter will set himself a task as experimenter which is way above the perceptual and/or cognitive capabilities of the human being. From the time taken by the pilot subjects, you will be able to work out how long the experiment proper will take and to see whether you have hopelessly under-budgeted (likely) or over-budgeted (unlikely) on this.

After you have, if necessary, modified the procedures in the light of the pilot trials – and done further pilot work if the changes were extensive – then you are ready to go, and the best of luck!

Experimenter effects

Many studies have shown that, if experimenters have an expectation that the results will turn out in a particular way, then they may influence the results by their expectations. The subject-experimenter situation is a social situation and it may well be that the subject attempts to please the experimenter by performing according to the experimenter's expectations, wishes or hopes. Thus cues such as tone of voice, brusqueness or friendliness, sharpness of movement, involuntary noises of pleasure or despair can all influence the results in the desired direction. The answer to all this is to standardize the procedure as much as possible and, if a situation appears to be one where experimenter effects could be serious, to use blind techniques, e.g. with the experimenter handing over the running of the experiment to some other person who does not know the experimenter's expectations or hypothesis. There are many fascinating experiments one could carry out on the experimenter effect itself.

Care and treatment of subjects

Subjects are precious things, as you will find out if you want to run an experiment with a large number of subjects from a particular population (e.g. male left-handers aged from twenty to thirty years). You must treat them properly. This means, amongst other things, telling them in as much detail as possible what it is they will be asked to do and how long it will take. If it is essential for the purposes of the experiment that subjects should be misled as to what it is all about, the wisest course is to seek the advice of a professional experimental psychologist. In any case, the subjects must be put in the picture as soon as possible after the experiment. Similarly, if you want to shock your subjects in any way – whether by electric shock or by obscene material – you must get proper advice before proceeding.

Remember also that many subjects will be rather apprehensive and nervous in the experimental situation and that it is in your own interest to get them calm and happy before you start. Finally, it is courteous to let your subjects know, after you have analysed the experiment, what your results were. People are fascinated by the results of experiments in which they were involved and it is in your own interest, if you want to do further experiments, to keep their interest well-stoked.

Writing up the experiment

Having carried out the experiment, you have next to analyse the results using those statistical techniques which you had previously decided would answer the questions that you are interested in, and which are appropriate to the experimental design.

It might appear that, having analysed and interpreted the results to your satisfaction, that is the end of it. But, no – if you have performed a worthwhile experiment, then others ought to know about it. Which brings us to the experimental write-up. Whether one is dealing with the first faltering experimental effort of the neophyte or the thousandth publication of the Nobel prizewinner, the objects of the exercise are the same. The main objects are to inform the reader about the results of the experiment, how they were obtained, and the relevance of these results. In other words, how do the results fit in with previous data and/or theories or with the theory presented in the write-up?

Suggested sub-headings for an experimental write-up

Whilst there is no one correct way of presenting an experimental write-up, the use of standardized sub-headings does help to provide a check-list to ensure that nothing important has been omitted. The following set of sub-headings is put forward in that spirit.

1 Title

This can usually be best given simply in terms of the independent variable and dependent variable, e.g. 'To investigate the effect of word frequency on recognition', 'The effect of overtraining on discrimination reversal', and so on.

2 Introduction

This begins with a general statement of the problem. It continues with a review of previous experimental work in the area and the explanations or theories which have been associated with the previous work. It then leads on to an operational statement of the hypothesis or hypotheses to be investigated. Some may prefer to have the hypothesis as a separate section, or as a subsection of the introduction.

3 Method

In this section, the reader is told exactly what was done in the experiment. The best way of deciding what should fit in this section is by asking the question – could the reader repeat the experiment exactly using the information given? It is useful to subdivide this section as follows:

a Design

A succinct statement of the variables in the experiment, together with their operational definition. The type of design (independent subjects, matched subjects or repeated measures) should be given, together with an indication of how subjects are assigned to conditions and what other variables are controlled.

b Subjects

State the number of subjects and give a brief description of the population from which they are drawn, together with the procedures used for obtaining the experimental sample. (In some cases you will be unable to sample, e.g. when the subjects are a laboratory class – if this is the case, say so.)

c Apparatus and materials

Any apparatus used should be described in sufficient detail for the reader to obtain the same. If the apparatus is available commercially, the manufacturer's name and the type or model number should be given; if not commercially available, details of construction and dimensions should be given. A fully labelled diagram is often very helpful.

Any materials specially prepared should be described here (e.g. sheets on which responses are to be made; jumbled words or anagrams).

d Procedure

This consists of a detailed step-by-step description of exactly what happened when the experiment was taking place. It should include all the things that happened to the subject between his coming in to the room and leaving it. Verbatim instructions should be given whenever possible. The way in which the stimuli are presented to the subject should be detailed, together with the way in which the response is made. Any time intervals imposed by the experimenter should be given (e.g. subject given a maximum of two minutes to recall the items; rate of presentation of slides was one per five seconds).

4 Results

The results should be presented as simply and clearly as possible. Make use of tables and of graphs and if, as is often the case, the analysis is concerned with the mean scores under two conditions, display these means very clearly. All too often such scores are tucked away almost out of sight. Any graphs should be understandable in their own right without reference back to the text, so they should be fully labelled on both axes, showing the units of measurement where appropriate. Remember that the convention is that the independent variable appears on the horizontal axis, the dependent variable on the vertical axis.

As well as the display and description of your results, this section should include the results of the statistical tests performed. An essential part of this is the significance level associated with the results of the analysis. A common fault of new experimenters is to quote the significance of the result and stop short at that – 'this result is significant at the 5 per cent level'. Remember that you are not doing the statistical analysis just for its own sake; you are doing it for the light it throws on your experiment. So you must go on from a statement of significance to explain what this means in terms of the experiment – 'this result is significant at the 5 per cent level, i.e. the mean time to react in the "alcohol" condition exceeded that in the control condition at the 5 per cent level of significance'.

It is not usually necessary to include all the experimental observations nor the details of the statistical computations in the body of the write-up. They can, however, be included as an appendix to the experimental write-up, which has the advantage that anyone going over the write-up can check up on details of computation and can help if you are making any mistakes.

5 Discussion

The discussion starts with the results of the statistical analysis and their bearing on the hypothesis or hypotheses that were put forward in the introduction. It then goes on to consider their relevance both in theoretical and practical terms. The way in which these results fit in with previous results is considered, together with suggestions for research leading out of the present work.

Limitations of the usefulness of the results should be considered here. It may be, for instance, that certain variables were, avoidably or unavoidably, left uncontrolled. The effect of this lack of control should be considered carefully. Be realistic about this. You cannot expect to control everything and just because, say, the wind changed direction in the middle of the experiment it does not necessarily mean that you throw up your hands in despair and say the whole experiment is worthless. There may, of course, be occasions when the lack of control of one or more variables does mean that the experiment is inconclusive. All that one can do here is to recommend that the experiment be re-run with appropriate changes. Even an experiment of this type is not a complete waste of time; it has at least made a contribution towards your education as an experimenter.

References

Any statements, theories, results or procedures which you have made use of in conducting or writing up the experiment must be given due credit. This is partly so that the reader can sort out the extent to which anything you say is novel or is derived from previous work, but mainly so that the reader is helped to find his way around the work already done in this area.

A common convention is to indicate all references in the body of the write-up by a name and date, e.g. 'As Craik and Tulving (1975) and Ley (1978) have pointed out . . .'.

The reference section of the experimental write-up puts all these references together in alphabetical order of the authors' names. Thus your reference section might read (in part)

Baddeley, A. (1981), 'The cognitive psychology of everyday life', *British Journal of Psychology*, vol. 72, pp. 257–269.

Gruneberg, M. M., Morris, P. E. and Sykes, R. N. (eds.) (1978), *Practical Aspects of Memory*, Academic Press.

Reason, J. (1977), 'Skill and error in everyday life',
in M. J. A. Howe (ed.), *Adult Learning*, Wiley.

For journal articles, as with the Baddeley article referred to above, the sequence is author's name, year of publication, title of article, title of journal, volume number and first and last pages of the article.

Some general points about writing up experiments

An experiment should be written up as soon as possible after the experiment itself is completed. This is important both in motivational and informational terms. If you are still 'involved' with the experiment, then the write-up will not be a chore, but will appear as a necessary wind-up to the whole process. It is in many ways a bad habit to write up experiments in batches. A great deal of information loss and of interference between experiments is possible with this approach. I have seen some fascinating examples of transposition of procedure between the accounts of one experiment and another. However full and clear your notes appear at the time of the experiment, leaving the write-up for a few weeks will often transform them into confusing hieroglyphics.

As far as presentation of write-ups is concerned, there is a lot in favour of a ring binder, particularly if you are carrying out a set of experiments. In this way material can be readily added or removed, the order of presentation of different write-ups changed, and so on.

It is also a good idea to have a look at some good examples of experimental write-ups. Have a look through books of readings containing journal articles. Alternatively, or additionally, if you have access to libraries possessing journals of experimental psychology, go and look through some recent copies: suitable journals would include *Journal of Experimental Psychology, British Journal of Psychology, Journal of Experimental Child Psychology* and *Quarterly Journal of Experimental Psychology*.

10 Conclusion

This book started out with the assumption that you intended to do experiments and had a problem which you would like to turn into an experiment, but you did not know how to go about it. Well, hopefully, you should now know something of how to go about it. However, one of the things which has not been discussed is how one goes about gathering problems.

Ideas for experiments

Probably the best starting point is observation. Observe the behaviour of other people, of children, of animals, of yourself. Why do I find it difficult to remember the names of people we have just met, whereas my wife remembers everybody's name? Why does the cat jump up to the kitchen window and hang precariously in mid-air with forepaws on the window-sill until the door is opened?

One could attempt to answer any of these questions off one's own bat. By careful observation one would pick out regularities and hope to get some ideas about what the variables might be. There is a lot to be said for this approach and, indeed, one of the most fascinating sets of experimental reports that I have come across came from a mother of six children who had carried out all her experiments on her own children and had attempted to convert naturalistic observations into controlled experiments.

However, although psychology is a young science, it does exist, and it would be foolish to ignore the previous work that has been done. How does one make a start, then? Any general introductory text will give you some ideas of the way in which psychologists have carved up the field. From this, using their references, you should be able to move to more specialized books and on to journal articles. A large proportion of the 'meat' of psychology is in journal articles, and you should get access to a library which subscribes to the main psychological journals.

Once you have a clear idea of the particular area you are interested in and some idea of the ways in which experiments in the area have been carried out and the theoretical approaches that have been used, it is a good strategy to switch the attack to the most recent work in the area. To do this, *Psychological Abstracts* is a valuable journal. If you look over the last two years for your particular topic you should discover several suitable references (one can sift through the abstracts very quickly). Looking up the references – and the references they cite – quickly gives one an idea of the main issues in the area. Your library may also have some form of computer search facilities. These techniques enable the searcher to go back in time. However, it may well turn out that a search of this kind turns up a reference which is absolutely central to what one is interested in, and it would be useful to know whether other researchers have followed it up.

This means going forward in time, and publications called *Citation Indices* enable this to be done. Here the index for a given year gives (amongst other things) the authors who, in their own articles, have cited a particular article.

The process is of course not simply one of checking up in the literature to find out if someone has already performed the experiment that you are interested in. As you read about the approaches which researchers have used and the results they have obtained, your own approach will be altered. What we are describing is a continuous interaction between your changing ideas and the ideas you encounter in your search of the literature. It may well be that, at the end of this process, you decide that the problem does not exist any more – that it is as satisfactorily explained now as it is likely to be for some time. It may be, however, that the experiments which you have read about seem to ignore something which you feel is vital. If so, go ahead, and do not be afraid of breaking out of the framework within which people are working in the area. It is very easy for people working in a given area to be unable to see the wood for the trees. They could be making unnecessary assumptions which you as a newcomer may well not share.

In this way you will learn a lot of psychology, you may find that the questions you are interested in have already been solved and you may, I hope, carry out some worthwhile experiments using the techniques covered in this book.

What to do if the techniques covered here cannot be used to answer the questions you are interested in

Do not despise the armoury of tests which this book provides you with. Very many problems can be quite sensibly attacked by considering the difference between pairs of means (*t*-tests) or of variances (variance-ratio tests). And if the normality and/or homogeneity of variance assumptions of the *t*-test cannot be justified, there are the non-parametric equivalents. Adding in Spearman's rho when we are interested in correlation and chi square where we want to test for association or goodness of fit, there are many more problems which can be tackled.

However you may find cases where the problem which you have can only be forced into a mould where one of these tests would be appropriate by altering the problem substantially. If you feel that this is unacceptable, then the best strategy is to seek advice from a (preferably psychological) statistician. You may find that experiments in the literature similar to the one you wish to run use analysis of variance techniques. In this case it may be possible to test your hypotheses adequately using *t*-tests on only two experimental conditions or between pairs of conditions (but remember the warning about significance level on p. 135).

What do I do next?

An experiment, and then another. And then some more.

References

Baddeley, A. (1981), 'The cognitive psychology of everyday life', *British Journal of Psychology*, vol. 72, pp.257–269.

Hays, W. (1973), *Statistics for the Social Sciences*, Holt, Rinehart & Winston.

Sidman, M. (1960), *Tactics of Scientific Research*, Basic Books.

Siegel, S. (1956), *Nonparametric Statistics for the Behavioural Sciences*, McGraw-Hill.

Underwood, B. J. (1966), *Experimental Psychology*, 2nd edn, Appleton-Century-Crofts.

Appendix 1
Using random number tables

Randomization is necessary at several stages of most experiments. For instance we might want to

(a) Select a sample of ten subjects at random from a population of a hundred.

(b) Allocate five subjects to an experimental group, five to a control group.

(c) Randomize the order of presentation of eight stimulus cards separately for each of ten different trials.

(d) Present pairs of random digits.

(e) Prepare fifty all-consonant nonsense syllable trigrams (i.e. 3 letter combinations).

The basic principle in randomization is to ensure that all the possible alternatives have an equal chance of occurring. It is unsatisfactory for the experimenter to try to generate random sequences by simply producing the alternatives in what appears to him to be a random order. There are for instance, strong number preferences. Random number tables (e.g. Table A, pp. 160–62) are very valuable – they simply consist of a large set of digits (nowadays usually produced by computer) in which 0, 1, 2, 3, 4, 5, 6, 7, 8 and 9 each have the same probability of occurrence at each position in the table. Providing that basic fact about the table is remembered, it is a matter of common sense to use the table so that it produces the kind of randomization required. One general point is that the table should ideally be entered at a random position ('pseudo-random' is good enough, e.g. stabbing a finger at it whilst looking away) and then movement from the point selected should be randomly up or down, left or right. The point behind this is that, if one always started at the top left-hand corner and went from left to right, then one would be ending up with the same sequence every time.

a Selecting a sample of ten subjects at random from a population of a hundred

Number the subjects in the population 0 to 99. Enter the random number table in a pseudo-random manner and use *pairs* of digits. Travelling, say, downwards from the point selected in the table, write down the first 10 pairs of digits you come to. Pick out the subjects corresponding to those numbers (NB the first 10 subjects in the population are represented by 00, 01, 02, 03, 04, 05, 06, 07, 08 and 09).

b Allocating five subjects to an experimental group, five to a control group

Let the even digits in the random number table represent the experimental group, the odd digits the control group. Again enter the random number table in a pseudo-random manner, but this time use single digits. Travel, say, left to right from the point selected in the table. If the first digit is odd, then the first subject goes in the control group, if it is even, then the first subject goes in the experimental group. Continue in the same way until five subjects have been allocated to one of the two groups; the remaining subjects go into the other group.

An alternative (simpler) procedure would be to spin a coin for each subject, 'heads' for experimental, 'tails' for control, again continuing until five subjects had been allocated to one of the groups and allocating the remainder to the other group.

c Randomizing the order of presentation of eight stimulus cards separately for each of ten different trials

Number the eight stimulus cards 1 to 8. Use random number tables and enter them in a pseudo-random manner. Travelling, say, right to left from the point selected in the table note down the first occurrence of each of the digits 1 to 8.

To make this clear, suppose that the line chosen from the random number table is

97 08 14 24 01   51 95 46 30 32   3③   19 00 14

Suppose we start at the circled 3 then, moving right to left, the sequence obtained is 3 2 6 4 5 1 8 7. Notice that 0 and 9 are ignored, as are second and subsequent occurrences of the digits 1 to 8. If necessary one would, of course, continue on the next line until the full sequence was obtained.

On trial one, then, stimulus 3 is presented first, then stimulus 2, then stimulus 6, etc. By continuing in the table, one can obtain a total of ten different sequences which will decide the order of presentation for each of the ten different trials.

An alternative procedure would be to take the stimulus cards themselves and to shuffle them thoroughly between trials. It is essential to shuffle extremely thoroughly, however (say two minutes of continual shuffling).

d Presenting pairs of random digits

For this, one simply uses the random number tables directly, entering the tables in the normal pseudo-random fashion and taking pairs of digits.

e Preparing fifty all-consonant nonsense syllable trigrams (i.e. 3-letter combinations)

If it is simply required to produce sets of three consonants where the consonants occur purely randomly, then random number tables can be used. One, of many, ways of doing this would be to code the consonants as follows:

B-00, C-01, D-02, F-03, G-04, H-05, J-06, K-07, L-08, M-09, N-10, P-11, Q-12, R-13, S-14, T-15, V-16, W-17, X-18, Z-19.

(NB Y is considered as a vowel-equivalent and is omitted from this list.) One enters the random number tables as before and, working with pairs of digits, simply notes down the occurrence of any of the code numbers.

For example, working left to right along the line:

64 <u>17</u> 47 67 87 59 81 40 72 61 <u>14</u> <u>00</u> 28.

The code numbers occurring are 17, 14, 00; hence, decoding, the trigram is WSB.

As you will have noted, a large proportion of the random number table is not used with this method, and a little ingenuity will provide a more efficient method. If, for instance, we were to again use pairs of digits but simply note whether the first digit of a pair is odd or even, then we could use the code

B-odd-0, C-odd-1, D-odd-2, F-odd-3, G-odd-4, H-odd-5, J-odd-6, K-odd-7, L-odd-8, M-odd-9, N-even-0, P-even-1, Q-even-2, R-even-3, S-even-4, T-even-5, V-even-6, W-even-7, X-even-8, Z-even-9.

Then with the same line as before, we can make use of all pairs of digits, e.g. 64, 17, 47 decodes as SKW.

NB There are lists of nonsense syllables which are scaled in various ways, e.g. for association value, meaningfulness, etc. Underwood (1966), p. 499, gives a useful list of sources of scaled verbal material of several kinds.

Appendix 2
Pearson's Correlation
Coefficient (r)

The main part of the text covered a correlation coefficient called Spearman's rho. This appendix is devoted to a second correlation coefficient known as Pearson's r; or sometimes as Pearson's Product-moment correlation coefficient. Whereas Spearman's rho is based on rankings, Pearson's r is calculated from the scores themselves. It is somewhat more laborious to compute than Spearman's rho but tends to be preferred by statisticians. It is also the basis for a number of techniques used in more advanced statistics.

The basic idea behind it is very simple. Table 1 shows two sets of scores X and Y, with the X scores arranged in decreasing order of size. The table also gives means ($\overline{X}$ and $\overline{Y}$) and, in the third and fourth columns the deviations from these means ($x = (X - \overline{X})$ and $y = (Y - \overline{Y})$) for each X and Y score. The final, fifth column gives the product ($x \times y$) for each pair of deviations. It is these 'cross-products' which are at the heart of Pearson's r.

Consider, as in the present case, where there is a positive correlation between X and Y; that is where high X and high Y scores tend to go together and where low X and low Y scores tend to go together. Now high scores will be above the mean and hence produce positive deviations which when multiplied together give positive cross-products (xys). But the low scores tend to produce negative X and negative Y deviations which when multiplied together also produce positive cross-products. So, for a positive correlation the sum of these cross-products (Σxy) will itself be positive, and if you think about it the higher the correlation the greater the value of Σxy.

When X and Y are negatively correlated however, high X scores tend to be paired with low Y scores (and vice-versa) which means that positive X deviations pair with negative Y deviations leading to a negative cross-product. Similarly negative X and positive Y deviations tend to be paired with a resulting negative cross-product. So for a negative correlation Σxy is itself negative. Similar reasoning suggests that with little or no correlation between X and Y the sum of the cross-products will tend toward zero.

So Σxy behaves in a way that we wish correlation coefficients to do and all that remains is to ensure that the coefficient falls within the correct limits, i.e. maximum value of $+1$ and minimum value of -1. The following formula accomplishes this:

$$\text{Pearson's r} = \frac{\Sigma xy}{\sqrt{(\Sigma x^2)(\Sigma y^2)}}$$

where $x = (X - \overline{X})$
and $y = (Y - \overline{Y})$

It is possible to test whether a Pearson's r coefficient differs significantly from zero by using Table C.

Table 1 Showing the calculation of cross-products (xy)

X	Y	$x = (X - \overline{X})$	$y = (Y - \overline{Y})$	xy
19	12	+9	+4	+36
14	16	+4	+8	+32
10	8	0	0	0
7	7	−3	−1	+3
6	4	−4	−4	+16
4	1	−6	−7	+42

$\Sigma x = 60$ $\Sigma Y = 48$

$\overline{X} = \dfrac{60}{6} = 10$ $\overline{Y} = \dfrac{48}{6} = 8$

Step-by-step procedure

Pearson's r

Step 1 Having listed X and Y scores in pairs determine the means $\overline{X}$ and $\overline{Y}$

Step 2 Determine the deviation scores (x) for X by subtracting the mean $(\overline{X})$ from each score

Step 3 Determine the deviation scores (y) for Y by subtracting the mean $(\overline{Y})$ from each score

Step 4 Square each X deviation in turn and find their sum

Step 5 Square each Y deviation in turn and find their sum

Step 6 Find $x \times y$ products for each pair of scores and find their sum

Step 7 Find r by applying formula

$$r = \frac{\Sigma xy}{\sqrt{(\Sigma x^2)(\Sigma y^2)}}$$

Step 8 If required, assess whether r differs significantly from zero by use of Table C.

Step 9 Translate the results back in terms of the experiment

Worked example

Pearson's r

X	Y	Step 2 $x\,(= X - \overline{X})$	Step 3 $y\,(= Y - \overline{Y})$	x^2	y^2	xy
12	7	+5	−1·5	25	2·25	−7·5
10	3	+3	−5·5	9	30·25	−16·5
9	8	+2	−0·5	4	0·25	−1·0
8	5	+1	−3·5	1	12·25	−3·5
7	7	0	−1·5	0	2·25	0
7	12	0	+3·5	0	12·25	0
6	10	−1	+1·5	1	2·25	−1·5
5	9	−2	+0·5	4	0·25	−1·0
4	13	−3	+4·5	9	20·25	−13·5
2	11	−5	+2·5	25	6·25	−12·5

$\Sigma X = 70$ $\Sigma Y = 85$ $\Sigma x^2 = 78$ $\Sigma y^2 = 88\cdot5$ $\Sigma xy = -57\cdot0$

$\overline{X} = 7\cdot0$ $\overline{Y} = 8\cdot5$ **Step 4** **Step 5** **Step 6**

Step 1

Step 7 $r = \dfrac{\Sigma\,xy}{\sqrt{(\Sigma x^2)\,(\Sigma y^2)}} = \dfrac{-57\cdot0}{\sqrt{78 \times 88\cdot5}} = -0\cdot69$

Step 8 From Table C, r must be greater than 0·53 for $N = 10$. As $r = -0\cdot69$ the correlation between X and Y is significantly different from zero, at the $p = 0\cdot05$ level

Step 9 This would be expressed in terms of whatever X and Y represent, stressing that the correlation is negative and differs significantly from zero

Appendix 3
Statistical tables

Table A Random numbers

```
03 47 43 73 86   36 96 47 36 61   46 98 63 71 62   33 26 16 80 45   60 11 14 10 95
97 74 24 67 62   42 81 14 57 20   42 53 32 37 32   27 07 36 07 51   24 51 79 89 73
16 76 62 27 66   56 50 26 71 07   32 90 79 78 53   13 55 38 58 59   88 97 54 14 10
12 56 85 99 26   96 96 68 27 31   05 03 72 93 15   57 12 10 14 21   88 26 49 81 76
55 59 56 35 64   38 54 82 46 22   31 62 43 09 90   06 18 44 32 53   23 83 01 30 30

16 22 77 94 39   49 54 43 54 82   17 37 93 23 78   87 35 20 96 43   84 26 34 91 64
84 42 17 53 31   57 24 55 06 88   77 04 74 47 67   21 76 33 50 25   83 92 12 06 76
63 01 63 78 59   16 95 55 67 19   98 10 50 71 75   12 86 73 58 07   44 39 52 38 79
33 21 12 34 29   78 64 56 07 82   52 42 07 44 38   15 51 00 13 42   99 66 02 79 54
57 60 86 32 44   09 47 27 96 54   49 17 46 09 62   90 52 84 77 27   08 02 73 43 28

18 18 07 92 46   44 17 16 58 09   79 83 86 19 62   06 76 50 03 10   55 23 64 05 05
26 62 38 97 75   84 16 07 44 99   83 11 46 32 24   20 14 85 88 45   10 93 72 88 71
23 42 40 64 74   82 97 77 77 81   07 45 32 14 08   32 98 94 07 72   93 85 79 10 75
52 36 28 19 95   50 92 26 11 97   00 56 76 31 38   80 22 02 53 53   86 60 42 04 53
37 85 94 35 12   83 39 50 08 30   42 34 07 96 88   54 42 06 87 98   35 85 29 48 39

70 29 17 12 13   40 33 20 38 26   13 89 51 03 74   17 76 37 13 04   07 74 21 19 30
56 62 18 37 35   96 83 50 87 75   97 12 25 93 47   70 33 24 03 54   97 77 46 44 80
99 49 57 22 77   88 42 95 45 72   16 64 36 16 00   04 43 18 66 79   94 77 24 21 90
16 08 15 04 72   33 27 14 34 90   45 59 34 68 49   12 72 07 34 45   99 27 72 95 14
31 16 93 32 43   50 27 89 87 19   20 15 37 00 49   52 85 66 60 44   38 68 88 11 80

68 34 30 13 70   55 74 30 77 40   44 22 78 84 26   04 33 46 09 52   68 07 97 06 57
74 57 25 65 76   59 29 97 68 60   71 91 38 67 54   13 58 18 24 76   15 54 55 95 52
27 42 37 86 53   48 55 90 65 72   96 57 69 36 10   96 46 92 42 45   97 60 49 04 91
00 39 68 29 61   66 37 32 20 30   77 84 57 03 29   10 45 65 04 26   11 04 96 67 24
29 94 98 94 24   68 49 69 10 82   53 75 91 93 30   34 25 20 57 27   40 48 73 51 92

16 90 82 66 59   83 62 64 11 12   67 19 00 71 74   60 47 21 29 68   02 02 37 03 31
11 27 94 75 06   06 09 19 74 66   02 94 37 34 02   76 70 90 30 86   38 45 94 30 38
35 24 10 16 20   33 32 51 26 38   79 78 45 04 91   16 92 53 56 16   02 75 50 95 98
38 23 16 86 38   42 38 97 01 50   87 75 66 81 41   40 01 74 91 62   48 51 84 08 32
31 96 25 91 47   96 44 33 49 13   34 86 82 53 91   00 52 43 48 85   27 55 26 89 62
```

Table A Random numbers (continued)

```
66 67 40 67 14    64 05 71 95 86    11 05 65 09 68    76 83 20 37 90    57 16 00 11 66
14 90 84 45 11    75 73 88 05 90    52 27 41 14 86    22 98 12 22 08    07 52 74 95 80
68 05 51 18 00    33 96 02 75 19    07 60 62 93 55    59 33 82 43 90    49 37 38 44 59
20 46 78 73 90    97 51 40 14 02    04 02 33 31 08    39 54 16 49 36    47 95 93 13 30
64 19 58 97 79    15 06 15 93 20    01 90 10 75 06    40 78 78 89 62    02 67 74 17 33

05 26 93 70 60    22 35 85 15 13    92 03 51 59 77    59 56 78 06 83    52 91 05 70 74
07 97 10 88 23    09 98 42 99 64    61 71 62 99 15    06 51 29 16 93    58 05 77 09 51
68 71 86 85 85    54 87 66 47 54    73 32 08 11 12    44 95 92 63 16    29 56 24 29 48
26 99 61 65 53    58 37 78 80 70    42 10 50 67 42    32 17 55 85 74    94 44 67 16 94
14 65 52 68 75    87 59 36 22 41    26 78 63 06 55    13 08 27 01 50    15 29 39 39 43

17 53 77 58 71    71 41 61 50 72    12 41 94 96 26    44 95 27 36 99    02 96 74 30 83
90 26 59 21 19    23 52 23 33 12    96 93 02 18 39    07 02 18 36 07    25 99 32 70 23
41 23 52 55 99    31 04 49 69 96    10 47 48 45 88    13 41 43 89 20    97 17 14 49 17
60 20 50 81 69    31 99 73 68 68    35 81 33 03 76    24 30 12 48 60    18 99 10 72 34
91 25 38 05 90    94 58 28 41 36    45 37 59 03 09    90 35 57 29 12    82 62 54 65 60

34 50 57 74 37    98 80 33 00 91    09 77 93 19 82    74 94 80 04 04    45 07 31 66 49
85 22 04 39 43    73 81 53 94 79    33 62 46 86 28    08 31 54 46 31    53 94 13 38 47
09 79 13 77 48    73 82 97 22 21    05 03 27 24 83    72 89 44 05 60    35 80 39 94 88
88 75 80 18 14    22 95 75 42 49    39 32 82 22 49    02 48 07 70 37    16 04 61 67 87
90 96 23 70 00    39 00 03 06 90    55 85 78 38 36    94 37 30 69 32    90 89 00 76 33

53 74 23 99 67    61 32 28 69 84    94 62 67 86 24    98 33 41 19 95    47 53 53 38 09
63 38 06 86 54    99 00 65 26 94    02 82 90 23 07    79 62 67 80 60    75 91 12 81 19
35 30 58 21 46    06 72 17 10 94    25 21 31 75 96    49 28 24 00 49    55 65 79 78 07
63 43 36 82 69    65 51 18 37 88    61 38 44 12 45    32 92 85 88 65    54 34 81 85 35
98 25 37 55 26    01 91 82 81 46    74 71 12 94 97    24 02 71 37 07    03 92 18 66 75

02 63 21 17 69    71 50 80 89 56    38 15 70 11 48    43 40 45 86 98    00 83 26 91 03
64 55 22 21 82    48 22 28 06 00    61 54 13 43 91    82 78 12 23 29    06 66 24 12 27
85 07 26 13 89    01 10 07 82 04    59 63 69 36 03    69 11 15 83 80    13 29 54 19 28
58 54 16 24 15    51 54 44 82 00    62 61 65 04 69    38 18 65 18 97    85 72 13 49 21
34 85 27 84 87    61 48 64 56 26    90 18 48 13 26    37 70 15 42 57    65 65 80 39 07

03 92 18 27 46    57 99 16 96 56    30 33 72 85 22    84 64 38 56 98    99 01 30 98 64
62 95 30 27 59    37 75 41 66 48    86 97 80 61 45    23 53 04 01 63    45 76 08 64 27
08 45 93 15 22    60 21 75 46 91    98 77 27 85 42    28 88 61 08 84    69 62 03 42 73
07 08 55 18 40    45 44 75 13 90    24 94 96 61 02    57 55 66 83 15    73 42 37 11 61
01 85 89 95 66    51 10 19 34 88    15 84 97 19 75    12 76 39 43 78    64 63 91 08 25

72 84 71 14 35    19 11 58 49 26    50 11 17 17 76    86 31 57 20 18    95 60 78 46 75
88 78 28 16 84    13 52 53 94 53    75 45 69 30 96    73 89 65 70 31    99 17 43 48 76
45 17 75 65 57    28 40 19 72 12    25 12 74 75 67    60 40 60 81 19    24 62 01 61 16
96 76 28 12 54    22 01 11 94 25    71 96 16 16 88    68 64 36 74 45    19 59 50 88 92
43 31 67 72 30    24 02 94 08 63    38 32 36 66 02    69 36 38 25 39    48 03 45 15 22

50 44 66 44 21    66 06 58 05 62    68 15 54 35 02    42 35 48 96 32    14 52 41 52 48
22 66 22 15 86    26 63 75 41 99    58 42 36 72 24    58 37 52 18 51    03 37 18 39 11
96 24 40 14 51    23 22 30 88 57    95 67 47 29 83    94 69 40 06 07    18 16 36 78 86
31 73 91 61 19    60 20 72 93 48    98 57 07 23 69    65 95 39 69 58    56 80 30 19 44
78 70 73 99 84    43 89 94 36 45    56 69 47 07 41    90 22 91 07 12    78 35 34 08 72
```

84 37 90 61 56	70 10 23 98 05	85 11 34 76 60	76 48 45 34 60	01 64 18 39 96
36 67 10 08 23	98 93 35 08 86	99 29 76 29 81	33 34 91 58 93	63 14 52 32 52
07 28 59 07 48	89 64 58 89 75	83 85 62 67 89	30 14 78 56 27	86 63 59 80 02
10 15 83 87 60	79 24 31 66 56	21 48 24 06 93	91 98 94 05 49	01 47 59 38 00
55 19 68 97 65	03 73 52 16 56	00 53 55 90 27	33 42 29 38 87	22 13 88 83 34
53 81 29 13 39	35 01 20 71 34	62 33 74 82 14	53 73 19 09 03	56 54 29 56 93
51 86 32 68 92	33 98 74 66 99	40 14 71 94 58	45 94 19 38 81	14 44 99 81 07
35 91 70 29 13	80 03 54 07 27	96 94 78 32 66	50 95 52 74 33	13 80 55 62 54
37 71 67 95 13	20 02 44 95 94	64 85 04 05 72	01 32 90 76 14	53 89 74 60 41
93 66 13 83 27	92 79 64 64 72	28 54 96 53 84	48 14 52 98 94	56 07 93 89 30
02 96 08 45 65	13 05 00 41 84	93 07 54 72 59	21 45 57 09 77	19 48 56 27 44
49 83 43 48 35	82 88 33 69 96	72 36 04 19 76	47 45 15 18 60	82 11 08 95 97
84 60 71 62 46	40 80 81 30 37	34 39 23 05 38	25 15 35 71 30	88 12 57 21 77
18 17 30 88 71	44 91 14 88 47	89 23 30 63 15	56 34 20 47 89	99 82 93 24 98
79 69 10 61 78	71 32 76 95 62	87 00 22 58 40	92 54 01 75 25	43 11 71 99 31
75 93 36 57 83	56 20 14 82 11	74 21 97 90 65	96 42 68 63 86	74 54 13 26 94
38 30 92 29 03	06 28 81 39 38	62 25 06 84 63	61 29 08 93 67	04 32 92 08 09
51 29 50 10 34	31 57 75 95 80	51 97 02 74 77	76 15 48 49 44	18 55 63 77 09
21 31 38 86 24	37 79 81 53 74	73 24 16 10 33	52 83 90 94 76	70 47 14 54 36
29 01 23 87 88	58 02 39 37 67	42 10 14 20 92	16 55 23 42 45	54 96 09 11 06
95 33 95 22 00	18 74 72 00 18	38 79 58 69 32	81 76 80 26 92	82 80 84 25 39
90 84 60 79 80	24 36 59 87 38	82 07 53 89 35	96 35 23 79 18	05 98 90 07 35
46 40 62 98 82	54 97 20 56 95	15 74 80 08 32	16 46 70 50 80	67 72 16 42 79
20 31 89 03 43	38 46 82 68 72	32 14 82 99 70	80 60 47 18 97	63 49 30 21 30
71 59 73 05 50	08 22 23 71 77	91 01 93 20 49	82 96 59 26 94	66 39 67 98 60

Abridged from Table 33 of R. A. Fisher and F. Yates, *Statistical Tables for Biological, Agricultural and Medical Research*, Oliver & Boyd Ltd, Edinburgh, 1953, by permission of the authors and publishers.

Table B Sign test

L = frequency of the less frequent sign
T = total frequency of *both* pluses and minuses

The table gives the highest value of L significant at the 0·05 level for each value of T (two-tailed test)

T	L
5	–
6	0
7	0
8	0
9	1
10	1
11	1
12	2
13	2
14	2
15	3
16	3
17	3
18	4
19	4
20	5
21	5
22	5
23	6
24	6
25	7

Table C Significance of correlation coefficients
(Spearman's rho and Pearson's r)

N = number of pairs of scores

The table values are the smallest values of correlation coefficient significantly different from zero at the 0·05 level for different values of N (one-tailed test).
For N greater than 10 the value needed for significance is essentially the same for either test.

N	Spearman's rho	Pearson's r	N	Spearman's rho or Pearson's r
5	0·90	0·81	11	0·52
6	0·83	0·73	12	0·50
7	0·71	0·67	13	0·48
8	0·64	0·62	14	0·46
9	0·60	0·58	15	0·44
10	0·56	0·55	16	0·43
			17	0·41
			18	0·40
			19	0·39
			20	0·38
			21	0·37
			22	0·36
			23	0·35
			24	0·34
			25	0·34
			26	0·33
			27	0·32
			28	0·32
			29	0·31
			30	0·31

Table D
The normal distribution

Fractional area under the
standard normal curve from 0 to z

z	0	1	2	3	4	5	6	7	8	9
0·0	·0000	·0040	·0080	·0120	·0160	·0199	·0239	·0279	·0319	·0359
0·1	·0398	·0438	·0478	·0517	·0557	·0596	·0636	·0675	·0714	·0754
0·2	·0793	·0832	·0871	·0910	·0948	·0987	·1026	·1064	·1103	·1141
0·3	·1179	·1217	·1255	·1293	·1331	·1368	·1406	·1443	·1480	·1517
0·4	·1554	·1591	·1628	·1664	·1736	·1700	·1772	·1808	·1844	·1879
0·5	·1915	·1950	·1985	·2019	·2054	·2088	·2123	·2157	·2190	·2224
0·6	·2258	·2291	·2324	·2357	·2389	·2422	·2454	·2486	·2518	·2549
0·7	·2580	·2612	·2642	·2673	·2704	·2734	·2764	·2794	·2823	·2852
0·8	·2881	·2910	·2939	·2967	·2996	·3023	·3051	·3078	·3106	·3133
0·9	·3159	·3186	·3212	·3238	·3264	·3289	·3315	·3340	·3365	·3389
1·0	·3413	·3438	·3461	·3485	·3508	·3531	·3554	·3577	·3599	·3621
1·1	·3643	·3665	·3686	·3708	·3729	·3749	·3770	·3790	·3810	·3830
1·2	·3849	·3869	·3888	·3907	·3925	·3944	·3962	·3980	·3997	·4015
1·3	·4032	·4049	·4066	·4082	·4099	·4115	·4131	·4147	·4162	·4177
1·4	·4192	·4207	·4222	·4236	·4251	·4265	·4279	·4292	·4306	·4319
1·5	·4332	·4345	·4357	·4370	·4382	·4394	·4406	·4418	·4429	·4441
1·6	·4452	·4463	·4474	·4484	·4495	·4505	·4515	·4525	·4535	·4545
1·7	·4554	·4564	·4573	·4582	·4591	·4599	·4608	·4616	·4625	·4633
1·8	·4641	·4649	·4656	·4664	·4671	·4678	·4686	·4693	·4699	·4706
1·9	·4713	·4719	·4726	·4732	·4738	·4744	·4750	·4756	·4761	·4767
2·0	·4772	·4778	·4783	·4788	·4793	·4798	·4803	·4808	·4812	·4817
2·1	·4821	·4826	·4830	·4834	·4838	·4842	·4846	·4850	·4854	·4857
2·2	·4861	·4864	·4868	·4871	·4875	·4878	·4881	·4884	·4887	·4890
2·3	·4893	·4896	·4898	·4901	·4904	·4906	·4909	·4911	·4913	·4916
2·4	·4918	·4920	·4922	·4925	·4927	·4929	·4931	·4932	·4934	·4936
2·5	·4938	·4940	·4941	·4943	·4945	·4946	·4948	·4949	·4951	·4952
2·6	·4953	·4955	·4956	·4957	·4959	·4960	·4961	·4962	·4963	·4964
2·7	·4965	·4966	·4967	·4968	·4969	·4970	·4971	·4972	·4973	·4974
2·8	·4974	·4975	·4976	·4977	·4977	·4978	·4979	·4979	·4980	·4981
2·9	·4981	·4982	·4982	·4983	·4984	·4984	·4985	·4985	·4986	·4986
3·0	·4987	·4987	·4987	·4988	·4988	·4989	·4989	·4989	·4990	·4990
3·1	·4990	·4991	·4991	·4991	·4992	·4992	·4992	·4992	·4992	·4993
3·2	·4993	·4993	·4994	·4994	·4994	·4994	·4994	·4995	·4995	·4995
3·3	·4995	·4995	·4995	·4996	·4996	·4996	·4996	·4996	·4996	·4997
3·4	·4997	·4997	·4997	·4997	·4997	·4997	·4997	·4997	·4997	·4998
3·5	·4998	·4998	·4998	·4998	·4998	·4998	·4998	·4998	·4998	·4998
3·6	·4998	·4998	·4999	·4999	·4999	·4999	·4999	·4999	·4999	·4999
3·7	·4999	·4999	·4999	·4999	·4999	·4999	·4999	·4999	·4999	·4999
3·8	·4999	·4999	·4999	·4999	·4999	·4999	·4999	·4999	·4999	·4999
3·9	·5000	·5000	·5000	·5000	·5000	·5000	·5000	·5000	·5000	·5000

Table E The t-distribution

(5 per cent significance level for two-tailed test)

DF	t
1	12·706
2	4·303
3	3·182
4	2·776
5	2·571
6	2·447
7	2·365
8	2·306
9	2·262
10	2·228
11	2·201
12	2·179
13	2·160
14	2·145
15	2·131
16	2·120
17	2·110
18	2·101
19	2·093
20	2·086
21	2·080
22	2·074
23	2·069
24	2·064
25	2·060
26	2·056
27	2·052
28	2·048
29	2·045
30	2·042
40	2·021
60	2·000
120	1·980
∞	1·960

Abridged from Table 12 of E. S. Pearson and H. O. Hartley, *Biometrika Tables for Statisticians*, vol. 1, Cambridge University Press, 1954.

Table F The variance ratio (F)

(5 per cent significance level for two-tailed test)

N_1 are the degrees of freedom for greater variance N_2 are the degrees of freedom for smaller variance

$N_1 =$	1	2	3	4	5	6	7	8	9	10	12	15	20	24	30	40	60	120	∞
$N_2 =$ 1	648	800	864	900	922	937	948	957	963	969	977	985	993	997	1001	1006	1010	1014	1018
2	38.51	39.00	39.16	39.25	39.30	39.33	39.36	39.37	39.39	39.40	39.42	39.43	39.45	39.46	39.46	39.47	39.48	39.49	39.50
3	17.44	16.04	15.44	15.10	14.88	14.74	14.62	14.54	14.47	14.42	14.34	14.25	14.17	14.12	14.08	14.04	13.99	13.95	13.90
4	12.22	10.65	9.98	9.60	9.36	9.20	9.07	8.98	8.90	8.84	8.75	8.66	8.56	8.51	8.46	8.41	8.36	8.31	8.26
5	10.01	8.43	7.76	7.39	7.15	6.98	6.85	6.76	6.68	6.62	6.52	6.43	6.33	6.28	6.23	6.18	6.12	6.07	6.02
6	8.81	7.26	6.60	6.23	5.99	5.82	5.70	5.60	5.52	5.46	5.37	5.27	5.17	5.12	5.07	5.01	4.96	4.90	4.85
7	8.07	6.54	5.89	5.52	5.29	5.12	4.99	4.90	4.82	4.76	4.67	4.57	4.47	4.42	4.36	4.31	4.25	4.20	4.14
8	7.57	6.06	5.42	5.05	4.82	4.65	4.53	4.43	4.36	4.30	4.20	4.10	4.00	3.95	3.89	3.84	3.78	3.73	3.67
9	7.21	5.71	5.08	4.72	4.48	4.32	4.20	4.10	4.03	3.96	3.87	3.77	3.67	3.61	3.56	3.51	3.45	3.39	3.33
10	6.94	5.46	4.83	4.47	4.24	4.07	3.95	3.85	3.78	3.72	3.62	3.52	3.42	3.37	3.31	3.26	3.20	3.14	3.08
11	6.55	5.10	4.47	4.12	3.89	3.73	3.61	3.51	3.44	3.37	3.28	3.18	3.07	3.02	2.96	2.91	2.85	2.79	2.72
13	6.20	4.76	4.15	3.80	3.58	3.41	3.29	3.20	3.12	3.06	2.96	2.86	2.76	2.70	2.64	2.58	2.52	2.46	2.40
20	5.87	4.46	3.86	3.51	3.29	3.13	3.01	2.91	2.84	2.77	2.68	2.57	2.46	2.41	2.35	2.29	2.22	2.16	2.09
24	5.72	4.32	3.72	3.38	3.15	2.99	2.87	2.78	2.70	2.64	2.54	2.44	2.33	2.27	2.21	2.15	2.08	2.01	1.94
30	5.57	4.18	3.59	3.25	3.03	2.87	2.75	2.65	2.57	2.51	2.41	2.31	2.20	2.14	2.07	2.01	1.94	1.87	1.79
40	5.42	4.05	3.46	3.13	2.90	2.74	2.62	2.53	2.45	2.39	2.29	2.18	2.07	2.01	1.94	1.88	1.80	1.72	1.64
60	5.29	3.93	3.34	3.01	2.79	2.63	2.51	2.41	2.33	2.27	2.17	2.06	1.94	1.88	1.82	1.74	1.67	1.58	1.48
120	5.15	3.80	3.23	2.89	2.67	2.52	2.39	2.30	2.22	2.16	2.05	1.94	1.82	1.76	1.69	1.61	1.53	1.43	1.31
∞	5.02	3.69	3.12	2.79	2.57	2.41	2.29	2.19	2.11	2.05	1.94	1.83	1.71	1.64	1.57	1.48	1.39	1.27	1.00

Abridged from M. Merrington and C. M. Thompson, 'Tables of percentage points of the inverted beta (F) distribution', Biometrika, vol. 33, 1943, pp. 73–8.

Table G Chi square

(5 per cent significance level for one-tailed test)

DF	x^2
1	3·841
2	5·991
3	7·815
4	9·488
5	11·071
6	12·592
7	14·067
8	15·507
9	16·919
10	18·307
11	19·675
12	21·026
13	22·362
14	23·685
15	24·996
16	26·296
17	27·587
18	28·869
19	30·144
20	31·410
21	32·671
22	33·924
23	35·173
24	36·415
25	37·653
26	38·885
27	40·113
28	41·337
29	42·557
30	43·773
40	55·759
50	67·505
60	79·082
80	101·879
100	124·342

Abridged from Table 8 of E. S. Pearson and H. O. Hartley, *Biometrika Tables for Statisticians*, vol. 1, Cambridge University Press, 1954.

Table H Mann-Whitney test

(5 per cent significance level for two-tailed test)

$N_B =$	4	5	6	7	8
$N_A = 2$	—	—	—	—	0
3	—	0	1	1	2
4	0	1	2	3	4
5	—	2	3	5	6
6	—	—	5	6	8
7	—	—	—	8	10
8	—	—	—	—	13

Adapted and abridged from H. B. Mann and D. R. Whitney, 'On a test of whether one of two random variables is stochastically larger than the other', *Annals of Mathematical Statistics*, vol. 18, 1947, pp. 52–4.

$N_B =$	9	10	11	12	13	14	15	16	17	18	19	20
$N_A = 1$												
2	0	0	0	1	1	1	1	1	2	2	2	2
3	2	3	3	4	4	5	5	6	6	7	7	8
4	4	5	6	7	8	9	10	11	11	12	13	13
5	7	8	9	11	12	13	14	15	17	18	19	20
6	10	11	13	14	16	17	19	21	22	24	25	27
7	12	14	16	18	20	22	24	26	28	30	32	34
8	15	17	19	22	24	26	29	31	34	36	38	41
9	17	20	23	26	28	31	34	37	39	42	45	48
10	20	23	26	29	33	36	39	42	45	48	52	55
11	23	26	30	33	37	40	44	47	51	55	58	62
12	26	29	33	37	41	45	49	53	57	61	65	69
13	28	33	37	41	45	50	54	59	63	67	72	76
14	31	36	40	45	50	55	59	64	67	74	78	83
15	34	39	44	49	54	59	64	70	75	80	85	90
16	37	42	47	53	59	64	70	75	81	86	92	98
17	39	45	51	57	63	67	75	81	87	93	99	105
18	42	48	55	61	67	74	80	86	93	99	106	112
19	45	52	58	65	72	78	85	92	99	106	113	119
20	48	55	62	69	76	83	90	98	105	112	119	127

Adapted and abridged from Tables 1, 3, 5 and 7 of D. Aube, 'Extended tables for the Mann-Whitney statistic', *Bulletin of the Institute of Educational Research at Indiana University*, vol. 1, 1953, no. 2.

Table J Wilcoxon test

(5 per cent significance for two-tailed test)

N	T
6	1
7	2
8	4
9	6
10	8
11	11
12	14
13	17
14	21
15	25
16	30
17	35
18	40
19	46
20	52
21	59
22	66
23	73
24	81
25	90

Adapted from Table 2 of F. Wilcoxon and R. A. Wilcox,
Some Rapid Approximate Statistical Procedures,
American Cyanamid Company, 1964.

Index

Index